T5-CVC-780

Selected Poems 1957-1987

Horst Bienek

PT
2662
.I39
A25
1989

Selected Poems
1957-1987

HORST BIENEK

TRANSLATED BY
Ruth & Matthew Mead
Eva Hesse

WITH AN INTRODUCTION BY
Hans Bender

Greensboro
Unicorn Press, Inc.

GOSHEN COLLEGE LIBRARY
GOSHEN, INDIANA

Copyright © 1957, 1968, 1976, 1989 Horst Bienek

Translation Copyright © 1968 Ruth & Matthew Mead
Translation Copyright © 1973, 1989 Eva Hesse
Introduction Copyright © 1989 Hans Bender

Cover portrait of Horst Bienek by David Hockney. All rights reserved.

"Boyhood in Gleiwitz," translated by Eva Hesse, first appeared in *New Directions in Prose and Poetry XXVI* (1973) and was reprinted in *London Magazine.*

Assistance to Unicorn Press during the time this book was produced was received from the North Carolina Arts Council and the National Endowment for the Arts.

Teo Savory, editor-in-chief of Unicorn Press, wishes to thank Anita Richardson and Erin Pearson of Universal Printing, Greensboro, for typesetting this book (in Baskerville High Density) and Inter Collegiate Press, Ann Arbor, for printing it (on an acid-free sheet); *designed by Alan Brilliant.*

Library of Congress Cataloguing-in-Publication

Bienek, Horst, 1930-
Selected Poems.

German and English.
  1. **Bienek, Horst, 1930-** —Translations, English.
  I. **Mead, Matthew & Ruth; Hesse, Eva**
  II. **Title**
ISBN 0-87775-206-0
ISBN 0-87775-207-9 (pbk.)

Unicorn Press, Inc. / P.O. Box 3307 / Greensboro, NC 27402

On the following pages of the "Table of Contents" we have identified the translator of the poems with capital initials, as follows:

MM ... for *Ruth & Matthew Mead*
EH ... for *Eva Hesse*

ZEICHEN UND SÄTZE

ZEIT UND ERINNERUNG

SIGNS AND PROPOSITIONS

TIME AND MEMORY

DIE ZEIT DANACH

THE TIME THEREAFTER

On Horst Bienek

Horst Bienek's *Gleiwitzer Kindheit* is the title poem of a selection of poems written over the time span from 1957 to 1985. Originally printed in literary magazines and anthologies, they were subsequently collected in occasional slender volumes. His very first poems appeared in the anthology *Junge Lyrik 1957* along with verse by leading representatives of what was then the younger generation—H.M. Enzensberger, W.H. Fritz, Christoph Meckel. Compared to his fellow poets, Bienek possessed the signal advantage of having undergone a traumatic personal experience that left its indelible mark on the whole of his work: his arrest and conviction by a military government court in East Berlin in 1951, followed by four years of detention in a labor camp in Vorkuta. His first book of verse, entitled *Traumbuch eines Gefangenen* (Dreambook of a Captive), published shortly after the 1956 anthology, was concerned exclusively with his personal experiences in the "silos of torment."

The *Gleiwitzer Kindheit* (Boyhood in Gleiwitz), in which Bienek relies extensively on his memories of boyhood, may be seen as a rough preliminary sketch for what would later become his longest and hitherto most successful novel, *Die erste Polka* (The First Polka). But it also stands in its own right as an independent poem in which the recollected scenes of boyhood are recorded in verses that owe their richness of imagery to the common idiom of the heterogeneous German and Polish population of Upper Silesia, in whose frontier town of Gleiwitz Bienek was born. This is evident from the outset in the opening lines:

> Memories of a winter woodland
> of Pistulka and his merry men
> of a turbid river sluggishly flowing
> of a Corpus Christi procession
> of the drunken shouts of the next-door Mainkas
> and once the local broadcast program
> interrupted by shots
> as the prelude to the great drive eastward

For Bienek this long poem also had the cathartic function of freeing him for a time from his obsession with the theme of captivity. Here he discovered a new subject and the courage to venture into "autobiographical verse." The sections of the poem headed "On the Klodnitz" and "The Road to the Mine"—"visions that appear in smoke and dream and flame"—are full of local coloring and aromas. Fateful scenes from the recent history of Upper Silesia are presented as flashbacks. Idyllic scenes alternate with glimpses of the realistic working-class background of the town with its coal mines and heavy industry.

The poem "Flucht, vergeblich" evokes memories of the year 1951 in Berlin, where Bienek had begun his career as a journalist while at the same time studying with Bertolt Brecht, who is deftly characterized in a few verses:

> In moleskin-suit, with peaked cap,
> pointed shoes, Virginia cigar
> that never went out

The scene switches abruptly forward into Vorkuta:

> The time
> between interrogation/beatings/lies
> and hopes.
> Lazarenian time/Butyrka time/Tundra time.

In his *Traumbuch eines Gefangenen* Bienek had treated the Purga in a separate poem untrammeled by statistics. It was a ballad composed of conventional quatrains, all in all a trifle too elegant. Terms like barbed wire, iron bars, rifles, bayonets, shots, hunger, excrement, death were either used as metaphors or woven into poetic images that were derived less from personal experience than from private reading. The more obvious influences are Oskar Loerke, García Lorca, Ivan Goll, Paul Eluard and even Paul Celan. Kafka has been regurgitated, Sartre is still being digested, Genet's *Querelle de Brest* has been recently discovered. And Bienek's motto "La réalité n'existe que dans la rêve" is borrowed from Proust.

In the slender volume of poems entitled *Die Zeit danach* (1966) Bienek overcame these original influences and abandoned the practice of stylized imitation. The impact of the poems "The Gathering" and "Accused" is more direct now that all ornamentation is eschewed.

Autobiography reappears in the cycle "Life Goes On," which contains a group of verses in which Bienek describes the red tape involved in getting his house built as well as recording some of the more satisfying stages of the work in progress. The closing verses of the new cycle—"In Australia"—brings us to the year 1975, when Bienek was "On the trail of Voss, real name Leichhardt." In the land "down under," Bienek discovered a wealth of new and unfamiliar words: "Words. Nothing but words." The most valuable treasures that a poet can bring back from a long journey.

Horst Bienek, who in earlier years himself interviewed so many authors on their tricks of trade and workshop secrets, has never as yet shown any inclination to analyze his own approach to writing. It might be said, however, that his poems are concerned time and again with poetological considerations. "Check every word/check every line" is his injunction to others and presumably also to himself. Elsewhere we read:

> I sit at the desk.
> I try to keep the words clean.
> A time which fights against the time.
> The shadows grow under the stones.

Bienek is neither an experimentalist nor a reductionist. He is at once complex, insouciant, and autonomous. Although he cannot be assigned to any specific literary grouping or style, his later poems manifest a certain kinship with the efforts of a few younger poets who in recent years have restored to poetry something of its original credibility, comprehensibility and applicability. This is particularly true of his autobiographical poems, which present experience and reflection in an idiom that is intelligible to a broad readership. The poet Wolf Wondratschek has expressed this succinctly in the observation: "Bienek starts out by recording biographical events and ends up with something that concerns us all."

Hans Bender

SELECTED POEMS

SIGNS AND PROPOSITIONS

ZEICHEN UND SÄTZE

Wörter

Wörter
meine Fallschirme
mit euch
springe
ich
ab

Ich fürchte nicht die Tiefe
wer euch richtig
öffnet

schwebt

Words

Words
my parachutes
I
jump
with
you

without fear of the drop
If you get the hang of them
you'll

float

Angeklagt

Angeklagt waren alle
aber nur einer von ihnen
bekannte sich schuldig
Die andern zerstörten der Stille Geräusch
sie verteidigten sich
aber sie verteidigten nicht ihre Städte
und nicht den lautlosen Vogelflug –
indes die Angst sie mit Messern blendete

Unschuldig aber war nur einer:
Der sich schuldig bekannte

Accused

All were accused
        but only one of them
        admitted his guilt
The others destroyed the sound of silence
they defended themselves
but they did not defend their cities
        nor the silent flight of the bird—
        for fear blinded them with knives

But only one was innocent:
He who admitted his guilt

Tundra

Äscherne Landschaft
Wo Trommeln verwirrn
Rostige Gräser,
Die im Eiswind klirrn.

Nie hat ein Mensch
Eure Formeln geschaut,
Nur einem Sterbenden
Ritzt ihr die Haut.

Im Tundramoos
Wächst ohne Saat
Bizarrer Urwald
Aus Stacheldraht.

Tundra

Landscape of ashes
Where drums bewilder
Rusty grass which
Clinks in the ice-wind.

None has beheld
Your formulae
You scratch the skin only
Of men who die.

From the moss of the tundra
Springs a bizarre
And unsown jungle
of barbed wire.

Der Mythos Zeit

Der Mythos Zeit zerbricht in Scherben
Die Vögel trauern sanft im Wind
Du hast den Kerker dir erwählt
Daß niemals soll die Wahrheit sterben
Du weinst und bist dem Traum vermählt
Die Vögel trauern sanft im Wind
Der Mythos Zeit zerbricht in Scherben

The Myth of Time

The myth of time disintegrates
The birds mourn softly in the wind
You chose the cell in which you sleep
That truth might live you passed the gates
And wedded to the dream you weep
The birds mourn softly in the wind
The myth of time disintegrates

Traumgaleere

Der Mond ist über den Strom gespannt,
In dem die Fische schlaflos laichen.
Die Sternenwinde sind verbannt,
Der Tag schickt seine Morsezeichen.

Es bringen den ersten Sonnenstrahl
Dir in den Kerker die Gewehre:
Durch diesen Vorhang aus blauem Stahl
Mußt du entfliehn. Die Traumgaleere

Führt dich bis zu des Zwielichts Saum.
Da falln im Hof bereits die Schüsse.
Du spürst das heiße Eisen kaum
Und hörst nicht mehr das Echo der Flüsse.

Dream-Galley

The moon is taut above the stream
Where sleeplessly the fishes spawn.
The starry winds are banished now,
The morse of day is heard at dawn.

In gaol you see the sun's first rays
Caught where the rifle-barrels gleam:
And through that curtain of blue steel
You must escape. The ship of dream

Conveys you to the edge of light.
And then the shooting in the yard.
The hot lead that you scarcely feel,
The rivers, echoing, unheard.

Der Toten Gebet ist kein Gebet

In *Workuta* wandelt kein Jünger des Herrn
Über die grünschäumende Tundra.
Hier gibt es keine Speisung der Fünftausend.
Hier stirbt an jedem Tag ein Traum
In noch ungewisser Frühe.

In *Workuta* rosten keine Maschinengewehre.
Wer müde ist, lauscht der Kantate
Des Schneesturms im Stacheldraht
Und stickt mit dem eigenen Blut
Mäander ins schwarze Katorgahemd.

Aber auch in *Workuta*
Ist der Toten Gebet kein Gebet,
Und die Lippen der Lebenden
Sind rostende Lippen, Gitterstäbe,
Hinter denen die Zunge eitrig verwest.

In *Workuta* steckt keine Witwe
Sich einen Schleier ins Haar.
Ihre Brüste erzittern noch,
Wenn sie an die Einsamkeit
Unter dem hohlen Leib eines Mannes denkt.

In *Workuta* gräbt keiner ein Grab
Den verwitterten Hoffnungen.
Und keiner ist da, der weint,
Wenn die ausgesetzten Toten
Mit der Schneeschmelze zu den Flüssen treiben.

Vorkuta

In Vorkuta no disciple of the Lord
walks the green-foaming tundra.
Here there is no feeding of the five thousand.
Here a dream dies every day
in the still uncertain dawn.

In Vorkuta, no machine-guns rust.
Whoever tires listens to the cantata
of the snowstorm in the barbed wire
and embroiders with his own blood
an endless pattern in his black katorga-shirt.

Nor in Vorkuta
is the prayer of the dead a prayer
and the lips of the living
are rusting lips, iron bars,
behind which the tongue festers and rots.

In Vorkuta no widow
covers her hair with a veil.
Her breasts still tremble
when she thinks of the loneliness
beneath the arching body of a man.

In Vorkuta no one digs a grave
for crumbling hopes
And there is no one to weep
when the abandoned corpses
drift to the rivers with the melting snow.

Ein Tag

Güterwagen Baracke Fischsuppe
der Marsch zum Ostrog
Filzung
    sagt man Brot und Arbeit
sagt man Sühne Strafe
    sagt man Tod und Tundra
sagt man und sagt man Stacheldraht
    und Schnee und Schmerz und
Purga sagt man und sagt man

A Day

Goods-trucks barracks fish-soup
the march to Ostrog
spot-check
          they say bread and work
they say atonement punishment
          they say death and tundra
they say and they say barbed-wire
          and snow and pain and
purga they say and they say

Katorga

Wer ist hier
        neben mir außer mir
Schatten einer Maschinenpistole Schatten
        Wladimir der Heilige
        alle Ursache und aller Anlaß
die Feuer verlöschen
die Silben sterben
        unter der Zunge
        das Wort zerfällt

Katorga

Who except
      myself is here beside me
Shadow of a machine-gun shadow
      St. Vladimir
      all cause and all occasion
the fires go out
the syllables die
      beneath the tongue
      the word crumbles

Die Schüsse des Mittags

I
Gegen Mittag fielen die ersten Schüsse

II
Ich liebe die magischen Formeln des Abends
Ich liebe die schwarze Sonne Tundranacht
Ich liebe die Flammengewitter der Frühe
Jetzt aber schmerz ich die marternden Schüsse des Mittags

III
Ich sammle Staub für die Toten des Mittags
um sie zu bedecken
damit der Himmel sich nicht erzürne
wenn er ihre Gesichter erblickt
Wer aber sammelt Staub für die Überlebenden?

IV
Verwandelt ihr Getroffenen
die marternden Schüsse des Mittags
in reifende Sommer
und es wird sein ein ewiges Feiern
und ihr die Könige
unter den zu Rühmenden

V
Die Ernte der Katorga hat alle Traumkammern angefüllt
Die Arbeiter vom Berge Ural sind aufgebrochen zur Rück-
[kehr
Öde und verwesend liegt das Land unterm polarischen
[Feuer

Shots at Noon

I
The first shots were heard towards noon

II
I love the magic formulas of evening
I love the black sun of the tundra night
I love the flaming storms at morning
But now I suffer the agonizing shots at noon

III
I collect dust to cover
the dead of noon
that the sky shall not rage
when it sees their faces
But who collects dust for the survivors?

IV
You fallen! transform
the agonizing shots at noon
into ripening summer
and there shall be an endless festival
and you the kings
among those to be praised

V
The harvest of Katorga has filled all granaries of dream
The workers of the Ural mountains have set out on
    their road home
The land lies deserted and rotting under the polar fire

Flucht

Flucht vor Steinen
      vor Regen
         vor Schüssen
im Fluß
versteint die Sekunde
      wer köpft den Himmel?
abwärts fällt er
      ein Schrei ritzt
die Erde
        sie blutet

Steine Regen Schüsse
im Windbogen
      im Schlafgehäuse
         in der Silbenkammer
und die Schüsse tödlich unsichtbar
        augenlos

Flight

Flight from stones
      from rain
            from shots

the moment
petrifies in the river
         who beheads the sky?
the sky falls
       a cry scratches
the earth
         earth bleeds

Rain stones shots
in the arch of wind
       in the shell of sleep
          in the chamber of syllables
and the shots deadly invisible
         eyeless

Aschenmorgen

Aschenmorgen
im Lid deines Auges gefangen
Landschaft
von Erinnerung verwüstet:

In die Netzhaut geritzt
der Schatten eines fliehenden Vogels
der Tod Arlequins
die Schrift der Reklamen
eine Flasche im lauernden
Grün des Absinths
und die unbemannten Schiffe
die heimlich deinen Atem verlassen

Aschenmorgen
läßt sich in deinen Augen nieder
und die sinnlos gezähmte Verzweiflung
wandelt in deines Bluts Labyrinth

Ashen Morning

Ashen morning
        trapped in your eyelid
    landscape
laid waste by memory:

Carved into the retina
the shadow of an escaping bird
the death of Harlequin
the lettering of placards
        a bottle the colour of absinthe's
            lurking green
and the unmanned ships
which secretly leave your breath

Ashen morning
settles in your eyes
        and the senseless tamed despair
        moves in the labyrinth of your blood

Das rohe Faktum des Todes

I

Niemand weint, wenn der Tag
Mit hartem Gelächter zerbricht,
Wenn die Angst furchtlos
Durch elektrisch geladne
Stacheldrahtwälder reitet,
Wenn verweste Fische
Mit stumpfschwertigen Rücken
Die Irrlichter-Carmagnole tanzen.

Niemand weint,
Wenn in den törichten Straßen
Und Linien der Untergrundbahnen
Sich die Blutgewitter entzünden,
Wenn Gomorrha und Dresden
Gefesselt über verwitwete Städte taumeln,
Wenn toxische Winde
Sich in den leeren Stuben versammeln.

Niemand weint,
Wenn Soldaten die letzten
Verschwiegenen Türen aus Rauch zerstören,
Wenn wir ausgeliefert sind
Den liebkosenden Messern,
Die vom Irrsinn genährte Ratten
Nach unsern entsetzten Blicken werfen.
Und nirgendwo regnet es. –

Niemand weiß, daß Tränen
Die Träume der Toten
In erhabene Abenteuer verwandeln.
Niemand weint schmerzverschwistert.

The Brutal Fact of Death

I

No one weeps when the day
Shatters with harsh laughter,
When dread rides fearlessly
Through electrically charged
Barbed wire forests,
When rotten fish
With blunt-spined backs
Dance the will-o-the-wisp carmagnole.

No one weeps
When storms of blood ignite
In the foolish streets
And the subways.
When Gomorrha and Dresden
Lurch in chains above their widowed cities,
When toxic winds
Collect in the empty rooms.

No one weeps
When soldiers destroy
The last secret doors of smoke,
When we are delivered to the mercy
Of caressing knives
Thrown at our horrified faces
By rats nourished on madness.
And it is not raining anywhere.

No one knows that tears
Change the dreams of the dead
Into high adventure.
No one weeps at one with pain.

II

In den steinernen Wäldern
(Vergilbt sind die Kehlen der Vögel)
Hallen nicht mehr die Schritte
Liebender.

Die Sterne, verwundet vom Klaggesang
Aus der Tiefe,
Schwimmen in gepanzerte Himmelsschächte.
Atomsicher.

III

Jeder Bruder ist Kain.

IV

Überall
Das rohe
Faktum
Des Todes.

II

In the stony forests
(Yellowed are the throats of birds)
The steps of lovers no longer
Echo.

The stars, wounded by the lament
From the depth,
Swim into armoured shafts of sky.
Atomproof.

III

Each brother is a Cain.

IV

Everywhere
The brutal
Fact
Of death.

Avant nous le Deluge

Sie wußten längst,
Daß kein Platz mehr für sie
In der Arche war.
Sie zogen traumentflammt
In die Ödnis der Berge
Und ließen sich dort
Als Fliehende registrieren.

Sie lehrten noch
Ihre Kinder das Beten,
Und daß es besser sei,
Auf dem Gipfel zu sterben,
Als unten im Dunkel.

Dann warteten sie
Auf das Steigen der Flut.
Sie wuschen zuerst darin
Ihre Füße in Demut
Und waren erschrocken,
Als sie erkannten,
Daß sie im Blut gebadet hatten.

Das machte ihr Sterben so furchtbar,
Daß sie im Blut ertrinken sollten.

Avant nous le Deluge

They had long known
That there was no room for them
In the ark.
They trekked ablaze with dreams
Into the mountain desolation
And registered there
As fugitives.

They still taught
Their children to pray,
And that it is better
To die on the peak
Than below in the darkness.

Then they waited
For the flood to rise.
Humbly they washed
Their feet in the flood
And were shocked
As they found
That they had bathed in blood.

That made their dying so terrible,
That they were condemned to drown in blood.

Sehr fern

Was geschah
geschah sehr fern
        einige von uns haben
        die Schüsse gehört

Die Urteile sind vollstreckt

        Auch wir standen auf der Liste
        Sie sagen: wir leben noch

Very Far Away

What happened
happened very far away
some of us
heard the shots

The sentences have been carried out

We too were on the list
They say: we are still alive

Vergeblich

Ich zeichne
in den Ufersand
          Buchstaben
vielleicht
ergeben sie
          Worte
vielleicht
ergeben die Worte
          einen Vers

Eine Welle
kommt
und löscht die Buchstaben aus
          pelt
          fschlag
     beharrlich ist
nächsten Augenblick
unter den Lagertürmen

Ich fange von neuem an

In Vain

I trace letters
in the sand
    of the shore
perhaps they will
    form words
perhaps
the words will form
    a verse

A wave
comes
and washes the letters away
        ble
        fbeat
     unwavering
    next moment
under the watch-towers

I begin again

König Odipus

Da stand einer
in der Nacht und
    er sagte man müsse
bewachen die Dunkelheit
damit keiner sie aufbreche
    Aber gegen sechs
kam die Sonne
und erschlug ihn am Hohlweg

In den Häusern zerbrach die Leere
die Asseln sammeln sich in den Rinnsteinen
und beschlossen den Aufstand
    (Die neue Regierung hob das Streikrecht auf)
der Palast war schon von Termiten besetzt
    keiner erreichte lebend den Ausgang

Da stand ein andrer auf
unbemerkt
und nagelte die Zeit an den Himmel
die Flüsse begannen
nach beiden Seiten zu strömen
    die Schatten
schifften sich ein
    nach Finis Terrae
im Gebirge aus Luft stürzte
vom höchsten Hauch Ikaros K. Düsenpilot
mit 177 Flugstunden
    ›. . . einer unserer erfahrensten . . .‹:
meldet die Zeitung
dazwischen: man nehme
    mäßig aber regelmäßig

Einer
tieräugig
steht in der Nacht und sagt
er müsse die Dunkelheit bewachen
damit keiner sie raube

King Oedipus

A man stood there
in the night and
      he said the darkness
had to be guarded
so that no one broke it open
      but around six
the sun came
and slew him in the defile

Emptiness crumbled in the houses
woodlice assembled in the gutters
and plotted revolt
      (The new government abolished the right to strike)
termites had already occupied the palace
      no one reached the exit alive

Another man stood up
unnoticed
and nailed time to the sky
the rivers began to flow both ways
      the shadows
embarked
    for Finis Terrae
in mountains of air
Icarus K. Jetpilot with 177
flying hours crashed from
the highest zephyr
      '. . . one of our most experienced . . .':
the press report
flanked by cures
      for night-starvation

A man
with the eyes of a beast
stands in the night and says
that he has to guard the darkness
so that no one steals it

Legende

Berg war ich einst
jetzt bin ich Fluß geworden
          ich fühl so alt wie Euphrat und Tigris

Als du noch bei mir warst
          beschworen wir gemeinsam die Gewitter
und alle Feuer
          die auf Erden wohnten
                    wandelten herbei
an Abenden die uns die
          Liebe fragmentarisch machte
du warst so seltsam dann
sprachst nur von Königen und Päpsten
und fragtest mich verwundert
          ob ich den Mond nicht auch
          gekreuzigt sähe?

Ich schwieg
und du hast in den Sand gemalt
Symbole

Dann taumelte die Sonne über uns
          verblutete im Mittag
          und schickte sterbend
                    Pfeile
in die Städte
du wolltest ihre Wunden stillen
          doch ihre stummen Schüsse
                    haben zehnfach dich durchbohrt

Legend

Once I was a mountain
now I am a river
    I feel as old as the Euphrates and the Tigris

When you were still with me
    we evoked the storms together
and all the fires
    that dwelt on earth
        approached us
in the evenings which made
    our love fragmentary
you were so strange then
spoke only of popes and kings
and asked me puzzled
    if I too saw the moon
    crucified?

I was silent
and you drew symbols
in the sand

Then the sun reeled above us
    bled to death at noon
    and dying sent
        arrows
into the cities
you wanted to staunch its wounds
    but its silent shots
        pierced you tenfold

Da schwieg der Stein
       wie alle Steine schweigen
Baum ging zu Baum
Wald wurde Wald
         und ich verbarg mich
    im Schatten
eines fliehnden Rehes

Berg war ich
      einst
jetzt bin ich Fluß geworden

Then the stone
      was silent like all stones
trees drew together
forest became forest
     and I hid
      in the shadow
of a hunted deer

Once I was a
      mountain
now I am a river
I feel as old as if I were
the Euphrates and the Tigris

Danach

Der graue Sommer ist hinter uns
die Stunde der Erschiessungen
Abschied
Vergessen

Jetzt können wir die einfachen Dinge
wieder einfach sagen

Afterwards

The grey summer is behind us
the hour of shootings
    farewell
    forgetting

Now we can say the simple things
simply again

Das Alphabet

für Nelly Sachs

Wo der Schmerz ist
      hat nichts anderes Platz
Er ist alles:
      es gibt keine Uhrzeiger mehr
      keine Münzen
      keine Gewehre
      keine Gebete
          Wind und Baum sind nicht mehr
          keine Farben keine Bilder
      nicht mehr Formeln
      nicht mehr Koordinaten
      keine Schlupfwinkel
      keine Zitate
      keine Feinde

Es gibt nur noch ein Alphabet:
      den Schmerz

The Alphabet

for Nelly Sachs

Where pain is
       there is room for nothing else
Pain is everything:
       there are no hands to the clock
       no coins
       no weapons
       no prayers
           Wind and tree exist no more
           no colours no pictures
       no more formulas
       no more coordinates
       no hiding-places
       no quotations
       no enemies

There is only one alphabet left:
       pain

In den Silos der Qual

Unbeweint
Schaufeln wir
In den Silos der Qual,
Wo seit Jahrtausenden lagert
Die Schuld der Lebenden,
Die Schuld der Gestorbenen,
Aber nicht die der Getöteten.

Unbeweint
Schaufeln wir
In den Silos der Qual,
Messen die Schuld:
Heutig bis ewig.
Sammeln sie, ordnen sie, schichten sie
In das Labyrinth der Schuldkategorien,
Die mit magischen Chiffren gezeichnet sind.

Unbeweint
Schaufeln wir
In den Silos der Qual,
Und nur für Sekunden
Straffen sich unsre gekrümmten Leiber,
Wenn wir mit erloschenen Händen
Sphinxene Ziffern an die Wände schreiben.
(Registraturen des Leids)

Und gebückt sehn wir nicht mehr,
Wie von Unbekannten
Immer neue Zahlen geschrieben werden,
Wie tödliche Netze,
Aus Plus und Minus gewoben,
An den Wänden erscheinen,
Koordinaten, Nomogramme,

The Silos of Torment

Unlamented
We are shovelling
In the silos of torment
Where the guilt of the living,
The guilt of the dead
But not the guilt of those who were killed
Has been stored for ages.

Unlamented
We are shovelling
In the silos of torment,
Measuring the guilt:
Now to eternity.
Collecting it, classifying it, stowing it
Into the labyrinth of categories of guilt
Which are marked with magic ciphers.

Unlamented
We are shovelling
In the silos of torment
And our bent bodies
Straighten up only for seconds
When with lifeless hands
We write sphinx-like digits on the walls.
(Registries of sorrow)

And stooping we no longer see
How new numbers are always
Being inscribed by unknown hands,
How deadly nets,
Woven from plus and minus,

GOSHEN COLLEGE LIBRARY
GOSHEN, INDIANA

Formeln, Gebete,
Mathematische Gleichungen von Schuld und Schmerz,
Kalkulationen von Sünde und Buße,
Qualparallelogramme.

Und manchmal läßt einer von uns
Die Schaufel sinken,
Geht durstig hinaus
Und kehrt nicht mehr zurück.

Wir aber schaufeln noch
Unbeweint
In den Silos der Qual,
Wohin wir verbannt sind
Von den Kommissaren der Vernunft.

Appear on the walls,
Coordinates, nomograms,
Formulae, prayers,
Mathematical equations of guilt and pain,
Calculations of sin and repentance,
Parallelograms of torment.

And sometimes one of us
Puts down his shovel
Walks out thirstily
And does not come back.

But we are still shovelling
Unlamented
In the silos of torment,
To which we have been banished
By the Commissars of Reason.

Exodus

Sie haben uns hinausgetrieben
In Nächten, da die Monde starben.
Geduldig trugen wir das Kreuz,
Das sie aus Lüge, Zwang und Folter
Uns gezimmert haben
Und unter ihren Kolbenschlägen
Brachen wir nicht nur dreimal zusammen –
Uns kam auf den endlosen Gräberchausseen
Kein Simon von Cyrene entgegen.

Wer unter euch Lebenden kann sagen,
Er habe uns gesehen?
Wer unter euch Toten kann sagen,
Er habe seinen Bruder erkannt?
Nur die Mütter ahnten
Hinter leidverhängten Fenstern
Unsern Auszug
Und von ihren Lippen flohn erschreckt
Gebete in das Dunkel.

Wir zogen nachtumstellt aus allen Städten
Und mit uns ging auch die Erinnerung.
Wir waren durstig,
Die Erinnerung hat uns getränkt,
Wir waren hungrig,
Die Erinnerung gab uns des Hiobs Speise,
Und wenn wir müde waren,
Hat die Erinnerung aus Disteln
Uns ein Lager aufgeschlagen.

Exodus

They drove us out
on nights when moons died.
Patiently we bore the cross
they had made for us
out of lies, violence and torture,
and beneath the blows of their rifle-butts
we broke down more than thrice—
On the endless road of graves
we met no Simon of Cyrene.

Who among you, the living, can say
that he saw us?
Who among you, the dead, can say
he recognized his brother?
Only our mothers
behind sorrow-curtained windows
sensed our departure
and startled prayers fled from their lips
into the darkness.

Encompassed by night we departed from all the cities
and memory went with us.
We were thirsty,
memory has quenched our thirst,
we were hungry
and memory fed us the meat of Job,
and when we were weary
memory spread for us
a bed of thistles.

Wir waren blind,
Die Erinnerung schuf uns die Illusion,
Wir waren taub,
Die Erinnerung war uns Musik von Cherubinen,
Wir waren nackt,
Die Erinnerung lieh uns des Trostes zweigeteilten Mantel.
Wir waren schuldlos
Und die Erinnerung ließ niemals uns
Vor Gottes Antlitz schuldig werden.

Sie haben uns hinausgetrieben
In Nächten, da die Monde starben,
Und ringsum blühte feindlich
Ein Wald von Bajonetten.

We were blind,
memory created illusion,
we were deaf,
memory was the music of the Cherubim,
we were naked,
memory lent us the divided cloak of comfort,
we were innocent
and memory never let us be guilty
in the eyes of God.

They drove us out
on nights when moons died,
and around us sprouted
a forest of hostile bayonets.

Resistance

I

Mit unseren Gebeten
Haben wir die Revolutionen verwirrt.

Ihr seid entflohn
Oder habt eure Brüder verraten,
Oder habt die brennenden Hänge verlassen,
Oder habt euch noch tiefer über die Reagenzen gebeugt,
Oder ihr habt geweint.

Wir aber schliefen furchtlos in den Feuern,
Uns haben die Flammen brennend vermählt,
Und der Gluthauch verschwiegner Bekenntnisse
Wohnte in unseren Augen vereinsamt.

Als wir erwachten,
Mischten wir uns unter euch.
Wir sprachen laut, aber keiner verstand uns:

Es war jene Sprache, die den stählernen Mittag
Zum triumphdurchbohrten Abend macht,
Die den Schnee und den vergeßnen Ballast der Fahnen
Schwartz von den Dächern stürzen läßt,
Die dem Verräter aussätzigen Zweifel schickt
Und die Sanftmütigen und Nachsichtigen
Beim Verkauf ihrer Tugenden überrascht.
Die Worte waren nicht mehr: Gedichte.

Sie waren: Geburt aller Dinge.
Sie wurden Fisch und Alraune,
Wenn wir *Fisch* und *Alraune* sagten,
Sie wurden Felsen und Blitze, Rehe und Trommeln,
Wenn wir *Felsen* und *Blitze, Rehe* und *Trommeln* sagten,
Sie wurden Asche und Heimat, Trauer und Zuversicht,
Wenn wir *Asche* und *Heimat, Trauer* und *Zuversicht* sagten.

Keiner kann sagen, er habe uns nicht gesehn:
Stacheldraht hat unsre Häupter geschmückt,
Bajonette haben die Formeln des Todes
In unsere Stirnen geschrieben,
Und die ungeduldigen Kugeln der Feinde
Sind seltsam in unseren Leibern erblüht.

Resistance

I

We have disconcerted
The revolutions with our prayers.

You escaped
Or betrayed your brothers
Or deserted the burning slopes,
Or crouched closer to your test-tubes,
Or you wept.

But we slept fearlessly in the fires
Wedded to the burning flames,
And the white heat of secret avowals
Dwelt in our eyes alone.

When we awoke
We mingled with you,
We spoke loudly but no one understood us:

It was that language which turns the steely noon
Into evening pierced with triumph,
Which makes the snow and the forgotten burden
Of the flags fall black from the roofs,
Which brings leprous doubt to the traitor
And surprises the meek and the indulgent
As they sell their virtue.
The words were no more: poems.

They were: the birth of all things.
They became fish and mandragora
When we said *fish* and *mandragora*,
They became rocks and lightning, deer and drums
When we said *rocks* and *lightning, deer* and *drums*,
They became ashes and homeland, sorrow and trust
When we said *ashes* and *homeland, sorrow* and *trust*.

No one can say he did not see us:
Barbed wire was our crown.
Bayonets inscribed the formulae of death
Upon our foreheads,
And the impatient enemy bullets
Blossomed strangely in our bodies.

Aber mit unseren Gebeten
Haben wir die Träume geordnet.

II

Wir sprechen laut, aber keiner versteht uns.
Doch wir wundern uns nicht,
Denn wir sprechen die Sprache,
Die man morgen spricht.

III

Ich aber frage euch: was habt ihr getan?
Ihr habt entrückte Mondlandschaften gemalt,
Und geweint.
Ihr habt in den Bars getanzt, in der Begierde Keller,
Und mit hochzeitlichen Lippen gesummt:
The song of the sweetest dream.
Ihr habt in den Zeitungen die Mordbilanzen gelesen,
Und geweint.
Ihr habt in den Untergrundbahnen
(Zwischen Babel und Vineta)
Vom Sein und vom Nichts gesprochen,
Und geweint.
Ihr habt das Toto zur Wissenschaft gemacht
Und die Wissenschaft zum Toto,
Und geweint.
Ihr habt scharfsinnige Diagnosen geliefert,
Aber keine Rezepte für Heilmittel,
In euren Büchern stehen große Worte
Über die Angst und über den Tod.

Aber unwürdig seid ihr des Todes,
Wo so viele würdig sterben.

IV

Niemand weint unter uns.
Niemand weint unter uns.
Niemand weint unter uns!

V

Mit unseren Gebeten
Haben wir die Revolutionen besiegt.

But we have set dreams in order
With our prayers.

II

We speak loudly but no one understands us.
But we are not surprised
For we are speaking the language
That will be spoken tomorrow.

III

But I ask you: what did you do?
You painted remote moonscapes
And wept.
You danced in bars, in cellars of lust,
And hummed with nuptial lips:
The song of the sweetest dream.
You read the murder-columns in the newspapers
And wept.
You talked in the tube
(Between Babel and Vineta)
Of being and not-being,
And wept.
You made football-pools a science
and science a football-pool
And wept.
You supplied clever diagnoses
But prescribed no remedies,
In your books are great words
About fear and death.

But you are unworthy of death
When so many die with dignity.

IV

None of us weeps.
None of us weeps.
None of us weeps!

V

We have conquered the revolutions
With our prayers.

Schwarzbitter Weiden die Studen

Schwarzbitter weiden die Stunden
Am Horizont der Qual.
Ich habe heimgefunden,
Verloren sind Rom und Baal.

Die Welt ist im Ungewitter
Der Gleichgültigkeit verweht,
Wo Kreuze ragen und Gitter,
Dort mischt sich ins Gebet

Der Börsenlockruf schon wieder
Und labyrinthisch webt
Der Wind die vergeßnen Lieder.
Sumpfmond sich taumelnd erhebt,

Verfolgt von erzürnten Chimären
Flieht er zu den Ruhlosen hin,
Die singend sich wollen erwehren
Der Einsamkeit Königin.

Gesang ist im Stern, in der Rose,
Musik gewittert im Laub.
Du weißt: die Metamorphose
Verwandelt auch dich zu Staub,

Verwandelt Fische in Bäume
Und Vögel in tropisches Licht.
Die Wahrheit flüchtet in Träume,
Die niemals ein Lächeln erbricht.

Bitter-Black Hours Are Grazing

Bitter-black hours are grazing
Upon the horizon of pain.
Rome and Baal are forsaken,
I have found my way home again.

The whirlwind of indifference
Has swept the world away,
Where bars and crosses tower
The voices of those that pray

Mingle with cries of the brokers
And wind, labyrinthine, weaves
Forgotten songs. The swamp-moon
Lurches up over the eaves,

Pursued by enraged chimerae
She flees to the restless men,
Who, singing, try to resist her—
Solitude's sovereign.

In the foliage music thunders,
There is song in the rose and star.
You know: the metamorphosis
Will turn to dust all you are,

Will change the fish into forests
And birds into tropical light.
A smile will never break open
The dreams to which truth takes flight.

Wenn man stirbt

Du wirst bald sterben.
Der Regen fällt schon dichter.
Vogelzüge stürzen
Im Zick-Zack in die Leere.
An den Brücken
Sind die Kontrollen verstärkt.
Ins Trommelfell
Werden Signale eingebaut.
Alle Wohnungen
Sind ohne Türen.
Der Regen fällt schon dichter.

Nur die Nacht läßt noch
Auf sich warten,
Sie sucht nach ihrem
Dunkelsten Gewand. –

Du wirst bald sterben.

When You Die

You will die soon.
Already the rain falls faster.
Flights of birds plunge
Zig-zagging into the void.
The guards on the bridges
Are doubled.
Signals are built
Into the ear-drum.
No dwelling
Has a door.
Already the rain falls faster.

Only night keeps you
Waiting for her.
She is choosing
Her darkest dress.—

You will die soon.

Unsere Asche

Stacheldraht
 ist der Mantel der Heiligen
wer mit Daunen oder Dunkelheit
bedeckt ist
 lebt in Sünde
Erst im Scheinwerferlicht
kannst du deine Schuld leugnen
erst in Verhören
 deine Tat verschweigen

Keiner spricht von den
vierzig Tagen im Hungerarrest
 (wer malte dir Tintorettos
 an die Zellenwand?)
keiner von deinem Weg
zur Abortgrube
 keiner hilft dir die
 Kloakenkübel tragen –
und unter ihnen
 brachst du mehr als nur
  dreimal zusammen

Niemand kam
 nur ein schwarzer Vogel aus Rauch
und später die Mörder
 erschienen pünktlich
sie trugen die Sonne
verwundet/durchbohrt/blutend
auf ihren Bajonetten
 zur schwarzen Wand

 Geh
sagte eine Stimme

Our Ashes

Barbed-wire
    is the cloak of saints
whoever is covered by down
or darkness
    is living in sin
Only when the lamp blinds your eyes
can you deny your guilt
only when you are interrogated
    remain silent

No one speaks of the
forty days on bread and water
    (who painted the Tintorettos
    on the wall of your cell?)
No one speaks of the path
to the latrine-pits
    no one helps you carry
    the latrine-buckets
and carrying them
    you broke down
        more than thrice

No one came
    but a bird of black smoke
and later the murderers
    appeared punctually
they bore the sun
wounded/pierced/bleeding
on their bayonets
    to the *black wall*

    Walk
said a voice

fünf Schritte zur Wand
und sieh dich nicht um
wenn die Schüsse fallen
Was geschieht
wenn der Schrei den Himmel kreuzigt
was geschieht
wenn der Wind die Erinnerung zerstört
was geschieht
wenn der Sonnenfisch in den Adern springt
und der Kalk unsre Gesichter auslöscht?

Die Antwort ist
schon ergangen
aber wer von uns
wer von uns hat sie vernommen?
Wer unter uns Lebenden
kann sagen
er habe sie gehört
wer sie gesehen –
wer von uns?

Wir haben Chlor in den Augen
Und Sand in den Ohren
und Ewigkeit
wächst lautlos in unserem Leib

Wann wird unsre Asche reden?

five paces to the wall
and do not turn round
    when you hear the shots
What will happen
    when the cry crucifies the sky
what will happen
    when the sun-fish leaps in the veins
    and quick-lime deletes our faces?

The answer has
    been given
but which of us
which of us has heard it?
    Who among us, the living,
    can say
        he has heard it
    who has seen it—
which of us?

We have chlorine in the eyes
and sand in the ears
and eternity
    grows silently in our bodies

When will our ashes speak?

Zeichen und Sätze

Rauch in der Luft
　　　oder Feuer im Meer
　　　oder Blitze im Wald
Zeichen von gestern

Wir haben sie vergessen
niemand sieht sie
　　　wir reden miteinander
　　　Worte
　　　oder Sätze
　　　oder Rauch
　　　oder Feuer
die Gemeinsamkeit der Worte ist der Satz
die Gesamtheit der Sätze ist die Sprache

Wir reden
sind eingemauert
　　　in Sprache
　reden
　　　verweilen beieinander
　　　im Dunkel
und das Moos wächst uns in den Mund

Signs and Propositions

Smoke in the air
   or fire in the sea
   or lightning in the forest
yesterday's signs

We have forgotten them
r.ᐟ one sees them
   we talk to each other
   words
   or propositions
   or smoke
   or fire
   the community of words is the proposition
   the totality of propositions is the language

We speak
We are walled-up
   in language
  speaking
   in the darkness

and the moss grows into our mouths

TIME AND MEMORY

ZEIT UND ERINNERUNG

Gleiwitzer Kindheit

I

Die Erinnerung an einen Winterwald
 an den Räuberhauptmann Pistulka
 an einen schmutzigen zäh dahintreibenden Fluß
 an eine Fronleichnamsprozession
 an das Säufergeschrei aus der Nachbarwohnung der Mainkas
 einmal auch das Verstummen im Volksempfänger
 Schüsse
kurz vor dem großen Krieg

Das ist alles
 ein paar Bilder
 aus einem überbelichteten Film
manchmal Schatten
 vielleicht ein Gesicht
 wenn ich lange hinstarre
eine Bewegung
eine Geste
 ein Lächeln manweißnichtvonwem

Ist die Kindheit Erinnerung
Oder die Erinnerung Kindheit?
Ich lese Borges und denke an das unerbittliche Gedächtnis von
 Ireneo Funes
 bei Sartre interessiert mich sein
 Verhältnis zu Descartes
ich möchte wissen was Coriolan dachte
 als man ihn gefangennahm

 Dann aber plötzlich
das Knacken einer Mandel
der Geruch eines bratenden Fischs in Bunzlau-Porzellan
der Schrei eines Eichelhähers im Labander Wald

Boyhood in Gleiwitz

I

Memories of a winter woodland
    of Pistulka[1] and his merry men
of a turbid river sluggishly flowing
    of a Corpus Christi procession
of the drunken shouts of the next-door Mainkas
      and once the local broadcast program
        interrupted by shots[2]
as the prelude to the great drive eastward

Nothing more
    just a few scenes
        from an overexposed film
sporadic shadows and
        if I peer hard enough
            perhaps a face
a motion
a gesture
        someone's smile

Does boyhood consist of memory
or memory of boyhood?
Reading Borges I am struck by the relentless memory
    or Ireneo Funes
      what interests me in Sartre
        is his reaction to Descartes
I would like to know what went on in Coriolanus' mind
      when they made him captive

      Then the sudden
cracking of an almond
the smell of fish frying in Bunzlau earthenware
a jay squawking in Laband Woods

Verwischte Bilder zittern über
          die Netzhaut:
Bergarbeiter auf dem Weg nach Hause
          Ein Karussel mit weißen Pferden und
hanfenen Mähnen
          Pfarrer Schewczyk eilt mit zwölf Ministranten zur letzten
Auf der geraden Straße nach Königshütte   [Ölung
          die Vogelbeerbäume von
Panzern geköpft im September
          und im Geäst verfitzt die Lieder:
Ich danze mit Djär innen Himmel chinein . . .

Schokolade auf Zuckermarken
          die Vitamin-Tablette
          als Hostie des neuen Reichs
zergeht langsam auf der Zunge
Späder schneiden wir aus der B. I. aus Erika und dem
Oberschlesischen Wanderer die Kriegsbilder aus
Und der Lehrer Skowronnek:
Nu kläbt mal de Bülder n eijre Häfle
und schraijbt von sägrajche Fäldzuck nach Polen.

Und wieder ein Wald und wieder ein Fluß
          die Klodnitz schwemmte den Tod nach Cosel
Und im Jahr 44
          sah ich die erste Leiche mit
          einem Schild um den Hals
sie wollte nach Breslau nach Köln oder ins *Paradiso*
der Hoppeck und Josel und Alfongs und ich
          wir standen am Ufer
          und pißten ins Schilf
ich wajss noch där Hoppeck hatte
          den grejssten Pullock
               du Dupa ich chab die Hedel . . .
          an dieser Stelle peitschten später die Schüsse
als sie die Gestreiften aus Auschwitz trieben

blurred scenes
    flicker across the retina:
    miners streaming homeward after work
  a roundabout's white horses
with their hempen manes
Father Schewczyk scurrying with twelve ministrants to a last sacrament
Along the straight road to Königshütte in September
  the army tanks sheared the crowns off the rowan-trees
interwoven in the branches a popular tune:
Ich danze mit Djär innen Himmel chinein . . .
Waltzing with you all the way to heaven . . .

Chocolate obtained for sugar coupons
    the host of the Third Reich:
    a vitamin pill
dissolving slowly on the tongue
later we clip war pictures out of the illustrateds
B.I., Erika, Oberschlesischer Wanderer
And Skowronnek, the teacher, urging:
now stick zee pitchers in yer copybooks
and call it see VIK-tor-rius Drife inta Polan'

Another wood, another river
    the Klodnitz bore death to Cosel
And in 1944
    I saw the first corpse
      with a placard attached to its neck
it was heading for Breslau, Cologne or Paradise
Hoppeck, Josel, Alfongs and me
    had been standing on the river bank
      pissing into the reeds
Hoppeck, I remember still
    had the biggest *pulok*[3]
      you *dupa*[4] you, I've laid little Heddy . . .
    at the same spot later there was shooting
as they drove the stripies[5] from Auschwitz

– warjanichweit –
das Bild erstarrt und ich seh einen Malerwagen
mit hohen Rädern
eine Hand zerbrochen zwischen den Speichen
Tote auf den Brettern
die Gesichter verdunkelt
mit Tüchern die Füße
mit Draht umwickelt:
dies Bild deutlicher als die andern: 19. Januar 1945

Noch deutlicher die Schüsse
Zerrissen die Bilder zerstört
die Gesichter
dann brannte die Stadt
wir gingen durch Flüsse wir gingen durch Wälder
wir gingen durch Schreie durch Fluchtprozessionen

Ich denke daran
während ich an der Kasse
für das neue Lichtspiel
eine Eintrittskarte kaufe
Lemmy Caution gegen Alpha 60

Ist Kindheit Erinnerung
oder Erinnerung Kindheit
was bleibt
eine Geste ein Lächeln das Streichen übers Haar
Fliegeralarm ein schuldig gebliebner Kuß
auf den man eines Abends vergeblich gewartet hat
ein Zimmer
angefüllt mit Leere
multipliziert mit Nacht
und heute mit deinen fünfunddreißig Lebensjahren
Bilder bleiben vielleicht Neurosen Bilder

—which was not far off—
in a flash I saw a housepainter's cart
with large wheels
  a dead hand sticking through the spokes
  corpses piled up on the planks
their faces covered with sheets
   the feet
   trussed with wire
this scene—January 19, 1945—clearer than the rest

More clearly still the shots
   torn-up pictures
     obliterated faces
       then the town in flames
we trekked through streams and woods
through cries and columns of refugees[6]

It all comes back
  as I queue at the box office
   to buy a ticket
for the new movie
  Lemmy Caution in *Alphaville*

Does boyhood consist of memory
or memory of boyhood
  what remains
  a gesture, a smile, a hand stroking a head
air raid warnings, a good-night kiss
  once waited for in vain
  a room
  filled with emptiness
  intensified at night
now, at 35, the scenes tend to linger
  as neurotic visions

Kindheit ist ein Film
der auf der Netzhaut des Auges abläuft
    überbelichtet
du schälst eine Apfelsine
    liest in der Abendzeitung den Bericht
      über den Absturz einer Boeing 707 am Fudschijama
      oder schreibst einen nicht ganz
        überzeugenden Brief an deine Freundin
plötzlich
in der Geometrie des Buchstabens
    im irrealen Schnittpunkt der Linien
      in der Explosion der Stille
die nichts als Stille entläßt
der lautlose Fall in die Kindheit
(es gibt keinen Sturz ins Nichts)
ganz tief
    ganz unten
      wenn du achtgibst
ist immer Kindheit
      wenn du deinen Brief nicht zu Ende schreibst
    den Bericht in der Zeitung nicht zu Ende liest
die Apfelsine nicht weiter schälst:
wirst du sie finden
    einen Lidschlag lang
      und eine Ewigkeit

Jeder Tag köpft eine Stunde der Kindheit
Laß dem Auge die Zeit
    und der Zeit die Verschwendung
der Güterbahnhof und der Dampf
    der Loks und der schmutzige träge dahintreibende
Fluß die Bergwerkstraße
    der Königsweg nach Przeskläbje
    ewige Kindheit
wo deine Bilder wachsen aus Rauch und Traum und Flamme

Boyhood—a movie
projected upon the retina
　　overexposed
you may be peeling an orange
　　or reading in the paper of a Boeing 707
　　crashing into Fuji
　　　　or writing a not wholly convincing letter
　　　　to your girl-friend
　　suddenly
in the geometry of a letter of the alphabet
　　in the fantastic intersection of the strokes
　　　　in the explosion of silence
　　in which only stillness is discharged
the hushed relapse into boyhood
　　(one cannot relapse into nothing)
deep down
　　at bedrock
there's always boyhood
　　　　if you do not finish writing your letter
　　　　if you do not finish reading the newspaper
if you do not go on peeling that orange
you will find it
　　for a wink
　　　　and an eternity

Each new day gnaws an hour off boyhood
Let the eye have time
　　and let time go to waste
the freightyard and the steam
　　the engines and the turbid, sluggishly flowing river
the road to the mine
　　　　to highway to Bezchlebia[7]
　　　　everlasting boyhood
with visions that appear in smoke and dream and flame

II An der Klodnitz

Die tausend Stimmen im Grund –
sagt er: das war ganz anders
　　　gingen hinunter zum Fluß
　　　stemmten die Arme
gegen den Wind
　　　brachen die flüchtigen Tore auf
unser Lachen
　　　schnitt Kreise aus der gläsernen Luft
das zersprang in Oktoberzeit
　　　aus dem Moos
schlugen die Flammen
　　　des Sumpfdotters
　　　: Totschka und Hus verbrannten:
Brennessel peitschten
　　　unsre wilden Knie
　　　Erdkunde mittwochs: Oppa Zinna Hotzenplotz
　　　Glatzer Neisse
wir stürzten ins Gras
　　　und zerrissen das Farnkraut
mit unseren Zähnen
der Sommer schmeckte nach Verfall
Ein Tag wie ein Jahrtausend
　　　bedenkt die Möglichkeiten: ist vorausgegangen: ein
　　　paar Schritte: Zyklen: richtungsweise: über die
　　　müde alte Klodka hinweg:
　　　　Und wie er auftaucht vom Schlunde
　　　　da war er müde und alt

Und starrten lang in den Fluß
　　　bis die Augen mitschwammen
weiter zum Westen hin
　　　ins Dunkel (weil das Schwarze der Anfang ist

II   On the Klodnitz

The thousand voices from the deep[8]
said: it wasn't like that at all
              and went down to the river
              arms stemming
the wind
       forcing volatile doors
our laughter
       cut rings in the crystal air
       which shattered in October
              the fiery tongues of the marigolds
dart
       from the marshland
       Totschka and Hus[9] burning at the stake
stinging-nettles
              lashing our wild knees
       Geography Wednesdays: Oppa, Zinna, Hotzenplotz,
       Glatzer Neisse
we flung ourselves onto the grass
              tearing at the ferns
with our teeth
the summer that year had a taste of over-ripeness
a day as a thousand years
       weighed the chances: went on ahead
       a few steps: cycles: sensing the direction
       way beyond the tired old Klodka[10]
              And when he rose from the deep
              he was grown old and frail

And gazed long into the river
       until our eyes moved with the water
further westward
       in the dark (blackness being

von allem)
und nicht mehr zurückkehren wollten
   die Wasservögel flogen
     den Kähnen nach
verirrten sich im Mittagsgerüst der Sonne
   im flimmernden Grün der Oder
   die heiter das Licht der Städte
sammelte
   tief unter sich begrub
     und erst im Ozean
   die Fische damit überschüttete
     und entlohnte
das flackerte: ertrank: erlosch: das gehört mit zum Ablauf:
zum Jahrtausend: *da zogen zwei rüstge Gesellen:*
   manche Kähne sanken
     schon vorher auf Grund
       sie hatten zuviel Kohle geladen
und zuviel Verzweiflung
     der Kohlenlader

Dann im Winter der Sternenfrost
     kam direkt aus Sibirien
   wie es Kotik vorhergesagt hatte
     und der Fluß knirschte
mit den Zähnen
bäumte sich auf im März
     wenn der Frühling
mit weißen Erstkommunion-Kleidern eröffnet wurde
     ließ die Brücken erzittern
und zerbrach unser Lachen
     aus Glas   Scherben
       zwischen den tanzenden
Eisschollen
   wir schrien der alten Klodka unsre zahmen Flüche nach

the beginning of all)

and no longer wanting to return
    waterfowl in flight
      tracking the barges
lost their way in the trellis of midday sunlight
    in the shimmering green water of the Oder
    which gaily gathered
the light of the towns
    diving deep down
      and on reaching the ocean
what flashed, drowned, died out: all is part of the process:
of the thousand years: *two lusty journeymen wending their way*
    many a barge had sunk
      in the past
        for having shipped too much coal
and too much despair
    of the loaders of coal

Then in winter the starry forest
    arrived straight from Siberia
  as foretold by Kotik
  and the river
ground its teeth
swelled in March
    as Spring came
wearing its white First Communion dress
    causing the bridges to shiver
  and shattering our brittle laughter
    into fragments
      between the bobbing
ice-floes
    we shouted at old Klodka our mild imprecations

Im Hochwasser ertrank
    unsre Knabenzeit
  jedes Jahr ein Stück mehr:
Zuerst der Bielschowski Antek im Frühjahr 37
Jontza Karel und Sczelski Hottek
das Jahr danach
und der Kryczyczek Josel im Februar 40
  ›der grüne Engel‹: weil ihn die Abwässer
  V.O.S.-Stickstoff für die Ewigkeit
    grün präpariert hatten
sein Vater war Blockwart in der Partei
    sang ›Deutsch ist die Saar‹
und änderte seinen Namen in ›Kreis‹
auf den Grabstein
  aber er ließ
›Kryczyczek Josel‹ schreiben
Mittwochs: Ohle Lohe Katzbach Bober mit dem Queis und die
Lausitzer Neiss: *Sein Schifflein das lag im Grunde*
    So still war's rings in die Runde
    und über die Wasser weht's kalt.

Gingen hinunter zum Fluß
    stemmten die Arme
  gegen den Wind
    schlossen die unsichtbaren Tore
    unser Lachen blieb
      zerfetzt im Schilf
    zerschnitt den Fluß
      – das grüne Gitter
senkt sich herab
    das Laub das mich bedeckt
      schmeckt bitter:
    ich hör' die tausend Stimmen im Grund

Our boyhood drowned
            in high water
        a little more each year
first Antek Bielschowski in Spring '37
        Karel Jontza and Hottek Sczelski
        the following year
and Josel Kryczyczek in February '40
                nicknamed the "Green Angel" because the liquid waste
            from the V.O.H. chemical plant had turned him that color
                for all time
his father, a Block Warden of the Party,
            had sung "Deutsch ist die Saar"
and changed his name to "Kreis"[11]
yet had them chisel
        "Josel Kryczyczek"
        on the headstone
Wednesdays: Ohle, Lohe, Katzbach, Bober with the Queis, and the
Lausitzer Neiss: *His craft lay at the bottom*
                and all around was calm
                a cold wind skimmed the water.

And went down to the river
            arms stemming
        the wind
            forcing shut the invisible gates
        our laughter
                torn to shreds in the reeds
        the green grating
            descends
to diffract the river
        the leaves that cover me
            have a bitter taste
        I hear the thousand voices from the deep

III Bergwerkstraße

Ich hör noch die Loks die Signale
    die Brücke das schläfrige Tier
rührte sich nicht
      die Güterwagen die Gleise die Licht-
Masten und die schluchzenden Dampfkessel
    neben dem Stellwerk die Schrebergärten
RAW ›der drittgrößte Rangierbahnhof Deutschlands‹
irgendwo dort
    im Gewirr des Anfangs
entsprang diese Straße
    der alte Bernsteinweg
      von Attilas Hunden
zuerst beschnüffelt
    von zahllosen Viehherden hart gestampft
    befahren von gebrechlichen Karren
mit laut schwatzenden Juden
    jetzt mit Schlacke unterlegt
    von den Vereinigten Oberschlesischen Hüttenwerken
gepflastert mit Steinen aus Ratibor
    und der Resignation invalider Grubjosches

Dort führte der Weg zur Schule
die Straßenbahn fuhr bis nach Morgenroth
    – *muj Bosche kochana:* dann hängten sie
Schilder auf: HIER WIRD NUR DEUTSCH
                GESPROCHEN
Die Vogelbeerbäume im Rauch der Frühe verhängt
    brannten am Abend im Märchenfeuer
    mit Totenaugen fuhren die
        Panzer vorbei
die Straße schwieg
    eingekreist im Gelächter der Lampen

III   The Road to the Mine

Still in my ears the engines, the signals
    the bridge a drowsy animal
    that never budged
        the freight cars, tracks, electric
    masts and the boilers chuffing
        allotments next to the signal cabin
the RAW[12]—"Germany's third-largest refitting plant"
    somewhere there
        in the confusion of the beginning
this road came into being
        the ancient amber trade route
        first scented
by Attila's hounds
    trodden hard by numberless herds of cattle
        traveled by rickety carts
with loudly jabbering Jews
    now laid out with slag
    from the Upper Silesian Iron & Steel Mills
topped with stones from Ratibor
    and the apathy of disabled miners

    That was the way to the school
the streetcars ran out to Königshütte
        mój Boże kochana[13]: then they put up
    those SPEAK GERMAN signs[14]
The rowan-trees in the morning haze
    glowed in the evening with fairyland fire
    the army tanks rattled past
        with dead eyes
the road remained hushed
        hemmed in by grinning lamps

die schwarz übermalt waren
und nur noch weiße Schlitze zeigten
das Reich übte Verdunkelung
die Straße schwieg
vorn schrieben sie auf die Lastwagen: SIEG
sie fragten mich nicht
wo die Straße endete
in Krakau Warschau oder Tschenstochau
(ihre Landkarten waren falsch)
– ich wußt es
sie führte direkt zu den Sternen
ich sah es
am Abend
vor meinem Fenster

Am Tag fuhr Molloy vorbei
mit einem Fahrrad
das rechte Bein war ihm steif geworden
oder wars das linke?
wars wirklich Molloy
oder Großvater Piechotta?
– egal –
wir gingen zur Schule
Geruch von Treber im Ranzen
Treber im Schwamm
in den Haaren
im Mund
vorbei an der Scobel-Brauerei
Geruch der uns taumeln machte
alte Frauen schleppten in Blechkannen
Einfachbier
Arbeiter stellten sich an für ihr Deputat
schwarz war das Bier
die Kohle
die Uniformen der Bergmannskapelle

now painted black to leave
        narrow slits of light
the Reich was observing blackout
        the road remained hushed
the SIEG[15] scrawled across the front of the trucks
        they never asked me
where the road ended
        in Cracow, Warsaw or Czenstochowa
                (all their maps lied)
                —I knew that it led
                        straight to the stars
this I saw
        one evening
                from my window

Molloy pedaled past by day
        on a bicycle
        his right leg had gone stiff
                or was it his left?
was it the real Molloy
        or just old gran'pa Piechotta?
—no matter—
we went to school
        satchels reeking of draff
the blackboard wiper reeked of draff
        as did our hair
                and mouths
on past the Skobel brewery
        old women trundling home
                carrying cans of small beer
        miners queueing for their issue of coal
the beer was black
        as black as the coal,
                the tunics of the Miners' Band

die Trauer der Witwen
    Die Kohle gibt uns zu frrässen
    und sie macht uns kaputt
war das Gebet des alten Piechotta

    Die Soldaten kamen
        die Straße entlang
            aus dem Mythos
des großen Reiches
    sie lernten mühsam unsere Sprache
    und sangen die Lieder vom Westerwald
und buchstabierten *Pjerunna*
    und fickten die Mädchen im Wald
nichts blieb: nur das Dunkel
sie wurden Witwen und ihre Leiber einsam und alt

Ich hör noch die Loks die Signale
    die Brücke das schläfrige Tier
rührte sich nicht
    in der Huldschinsky-Siedlung Geschrei
Streit mit dem Messer
    und die Lieder
der Prozession zum Kalvarienberg
    die Worte erstarren im Frost
    – der du wurdest von deinem Jünger verraten
    – der du wurdest gestäupt und gefoltert
    – der du wurdest ans Kreuz geschlagen

Jede Straße führt in die Kindheit
    aber ich weiß
        die Bergwerkstraße
führt zu den Sternen
    am letzten Tag
werd ich sie wiederfinden

and the widows' weeds
> *The coal bringeth sustenance*
> *and killeth into the bargain*
thus the prayer of old Piechotta

Troops
>> moving along the road
>>> straight out of the myth
of the Third Reich
>> they had trouble with our lingo
>> and sang songs of the Westerwald
and spelled out *Perunnja*[16]
>>> and laid our girls in the wood
>>> and nothing now is left but the blackness
they became widows with bodies lonely and aged

Still in my ear the sound of the engines, the signals
>> the bridge a drowsy animal
>> that never budged
>>> shouts from the Huldschinsky settlement
>> a carve-up with knives
>>> and the hymns
the procession to Calvary[17]
>>> the words freeze in the cold air
>>> — Thou who wert betrayed by thy disciple
>>> — Thou who wert scourged and tortured
>>> — Thou who wert nailed to the Cross

Every road leads back to boyhood
>> but the road to the mine
>>> this I know
leads to heaven
>> when doomsday comes
>> I shall tread you once again

IV

Jeder Tag köpft eine Stunde der Kindheit
— ich rück näher den Stuhl
an den Schreibtisch heran
rauch eine Marlboro
die Bilder erzittern auf meiner Netzhaut
verwischen
ich will sie festhalten
ich schreibe:
der Güterbahnhof und der Dampf
der Loks und der schmutzige
träge dahintreibende Fluß
die tausend Stimmen im Grund
die Bergwerkstraße
der Königsweg nach Przeskläbje
ewige Kindheit
wo deine Bilder wachsen aus Rauch und Traum und Flamme

IV

Each new day gnaws an hour off boyhood
     — I move my chair
     nearer to the writing desk
     draw on a Marlboro
the scenes flicker across my retina
     and then fade out of focus
     For the record
        I jot down:
freight-yard, the steam
engines, the turbid
sluggishly flowing river
     the thousand voices from the deep
the road to the mine
     the highway to Bezchlebia
     everlasting boyhood
the visions that appear in smoke and dream and flame

Gedicht von Zeit und Erinnerung

I

Sie sagen: Erinnerung hat Dauer
sie sagen: Kunst währt ewig
Der Marmor splittert
und der Ruhm verwest
das wissen wir
das Weiche zerstört das Harte
das ist so alt wie die Welt

Atem ist Leben und Stillstand Tod
Stillstand ist aber auch Immer
ist Ewigkeit
ist von Dauer
ist dann Ewigkeit Tod?
Alles was sich bewegt
läßt sich verändern
was in unserm Gedächtnis erstarrt
nicht mehr
ist für die Dauer bestimmt
aber wer will entscheiden was dauerhafter ist:
der geometrische Flug der Taube
der steile Sprung des Tänzers
der traumlose Schlaf der Katze
die labyrinthische Konstruktion des Computers

Immer wetteifert die Vollkommenheit mit der Zerstörung
die Magnolie duftet am stärksten
wenn sie stirbt
der Traum wird dann Wirklichkeit
wenn dich die Schüsse durchbohrn
(alle werden teilhaben an diesem Traum
aber keiner wird darüber sprechen
die überleben werden sich ihre Narben zeigen
und einander zunickend / schweigend / weitergehn)

Poem of Time and Memory

I

Memory, they say, endures
    Art, they say, lasts forever
Marble gets chipped
    and fame fades
        that we know
the soft destroys the hard
    as it always has since the world began

Breath is life, standstill is death
    but standstill is forever
    is eternity
it endures
        is then eternity death?
    All that moves
can be changed
    all that takes root in memory
    can not
        it is ordained to last
but who shall decide what is more abiding:
the geometrical flight of the dove
the vertical leap of the dancer
the dreamless sleep of the cat
the labyrinthine circuit of the computer

Perfection is forever contending with destruction
    never is the magnolia more fragrant
than when it is dying
    the dream becomes reality
as the bullets enter your body
(this dream will be shared by all
though none will talk about it
the survivors will show each other their scars
and, with a silent nod, continue on their way)

II
Dir bleibt nichts
du gehst über eine Brücke und der Fluß hält nicht an
du betest vor einer Madonna und das Wunder geschieht nicht
du spuckst in die Sonne und das Feuer erlischt nicht
(das wär was)
was ist von Dauer:
    die Buchstabenkolonnen auf weißem Papier
die Rechnungsergebnisse   Marketing
    A lume spento   das Portrait von B.   Kif
das Schachspiel   Trauer   ein Gespräch im Flugzeug
    eau de vie de poire   der Beischlaf
            die Erinnerung daran
ist von Dauer
    ich sag es ja ich sags ja
darüber entscheiden wir nicht

Mein Gott wenn ich das höre
    nein besser nicht das kennen wir
immer dasselbe
        am besten schweigen
            aufhören
    die Zeit der Balladen ist vorbei
der großen Formen
der Manifeste (das kennen wir)
Memphis zerfiel
    Warschau wurde zerstört
    Gleiwitz brannte unterm Schnee
        die Zeit erstarrt
in unaufhörlicher Bewegung und nichts ist
was nicht war und sein wird
Wenn das Ende naht sagt Borges
    bleiben von der Erinnerung keine Bilder mehr
was allein bleibt sind Worte

II

Nothing will be left for you
when you pass over a bridge the water will not stop flowing
when you pray to a madonna no miracle will be forthcoming
when you spit at the sun its fire will not be quenched
(that would be something)
what endures
 columns of print on white paper
statistics marketing
  A lume spento the portrait of B. Kif
the game of chess grief a conversation in a plane
  eau de vie de poire copulation
    the memory
endures
 it's just as I say, just as I say
it's not up to us

My God, when I hear that
 no, better not, we know all that
always the same thing
  better to shut up
  to be quiet
  the age of the ballad is dead and gone
the major forms
the manifestoes (we know all this)
Memphis crumbled
  Warsaw was destroyed
  Gleiwitz burnt down under the snow
  time is locked
in perpetual motion, nothing exists
that was not here before or will not come again
As the end approaches, Borges says,
 the memory is drained of images
nothing is left but words

III

Zwanzig Jahre mußten vergehen Zeitvergangenheit
     bis in Frankfurt Gerichtstag gehalten wurde
über das Totenhaus dieser Welt
ARBEIT MACHT FREI / DIE IHR EINTRETET / FIN DE PARTIE
(das ist ein und dasselbe)
: eingeritzt in die Haut der Lebenden
versenkt in die Abortgruben der Lager
vermischt mit dem Rauch der Krematorien
     mit dem *ersten Atem* der Neugebornen
ist es von Dauer
     soll es von Dauer sein
          wird es von Dauer sein

     Nicht die Geschichte hat Dauer
          die Gegenwart
und was von der Geschichte
noch Gegenwart ist
zürnt ihm nicht dem Aufschreiber
     wenn er
stammelt wenn er von vorn anfängt:

Das ist der Anfang:
das Wort ist ein Wort und das Bild ist ein Bild und der Satz
ist ein Satz
          und schwarz ist nichts
andres als schwarz und rot nichts andres als rot
und Leben bedeutet nicht
          tausend Möglichkeiten zu sterben
sondern da zu sein

Nicht das was war hat Dauer
Nur das was ist
               was sein wird

III

Twenty years had to elapse. The time lag
        before the Frankfurt court passed its verdict
on the mortuary of the world
ARBEIT MACHT FREI /ALL YE WHO ENTER HERE/ FIN DE PARTIE
(it all means one and the same)
tattooed on the skin of the living
sunk in the cesspools of the camps
mixed with the smoke of the crematoriums
        with the *first breath* of the newborn
if it is to endure
        if it is intended to endure
                then it will endure

        It is not history that endures
        but the present
and what in history
is still of the present
don't lose patience with the chronicler
        if he
stutters as he begins at the beginning:

That is the beginning:
the word is a word and the image is an image and the proposition
is a proposition
                and black is nothing
but black, red nothing but red
and the meaning of life
        is not a thousand ways of dying
but being present
What endures is not what was
but solely what is
                        what will be

THE TIME THEREAFTER

DIE ZEIT DANACH

Sagen Schweigen Sagen

Wenn wir alles gesagt haben werden
wird immer noch etwas zu sagen sein
wenn noch etwas zu sagen ist
werden wir nicht aufhören dürfen
zu sagen was zu sagen ist
wenn wir anfangen werden zu schweigen
werden andere über uns sagen
was zu sagen ist
so wird nicht aufhören
das Sagen und Sagen über das Sagen

Ohne das Sagen gibt es nichts
wenn ich nicht das
was geschehen ist
sage erzähle oder beschreibe
ist das Geschehen
überhaupt nicht geschehen
das Sagen wird fortgesetzt
Stück für Stück
besser: Bruchstück für Bruchstück

Niemals wird es das Ganze sein
niemals also wird alles gesagt sein

Saying Not Saying Saying

When we have said all
there will always remain more to be said
if there is still something to be said
we shall not be permitted to stop
saying what has to be said
once we begin to keep silent
others will say of us
what is to be said
so there will be no end to
saying and saying about saying

But for the saying nothing exists
if I do not
say narrate describe
what has happened
then the happening
will never really have happened
the saying continues
bit by bit
or rather: bite by bite

It will never come to an end
so never will all be said

Schattensprache

Ich rede nicht vom Sieg
        weil ich Niederlagen erlitten habe
ich spreche nicht von der Schönheit
        weil mein Körper mit Narben bedeckt ist
ich weigere mich den Gesang zu rühmen
        weil meine Kehle verstummt ist
ich setze die Worte nebeneinander
        weil ich schweigen möchte
ich spreche die Sätze vor
        weil ich ihr Wesen angeben will
Das Wesen des Satzes angeben
heißt das Wesen aller Beschreibung angeben
also das Wesen der Welt
die Sprache folgt mir nach
        ist immer hinter mir
Schattensprache

Shadow Language

I will not speak of victory
    for I have suffered reverses
I will not speak of beauty
    for my body is covered with scars
I refuse to celebrate song
    for my voice sticks in my throat
I arrange words in parataxis
    for I would keep silent
I recite the propositions
    for I would give their essence
To give the essence of a proposition
means to give the essence of all description
and thus the essence of the world
Language dogs me
    trailing forever behind me
umbralingua

Gartenfest

Spät in der Nacht
wenn die Kerzen
in den Lampions abgebrannt sind
wenn die aufgehängten Gesichter
im Dunkel verschwinden
die Musiker mit dem Bus weggefahren sind
die Kellner die Tische abräumen
und die leeren Worthülsen zusammenkehren
wenn die letzten Grillfeuer erlöschen

Stürzen lautlos gefällt
im Park die Bäume
Schatten füllt die Gläser
der Zurückgebliebenen
Wir trinken daraus
Gelächter steigt in uns auf
wir gehn ein paar Schritte
wir tanzen

Verwundert schaun die Lebenden uns zu

Garden Party

Late at night
when the wicks
have burnt out in the Chinese lanterns
when the suspended faces
fade into the darkness
when the musicians have left by coach
the waiters clear away the tables
and sweep up the empty husks of words
as the last barbecue fires peter out

The trees in the park
are silently felled
shadow fills the glasses
of the remaining guests
As we drink
laughter rises up within us
we walk a few steps
we dance

The living regard us with wonder

Der besiegte Sieger

Ich komme nicht allein
mit mir sind viele
    wir durchkämmen die Wälder
    wir überqueren die Flüsse
    wir setzen ihre Schiffe in Brand
    wir sprengen ihre unterirdischen Tunnelsysteme
    wir besetzen die Stadt
        sie ergeben sich kampflos
    wir nehmen ihnen die Waffen
        sie wehren sich nicht
    wir beschlagnahmen ihre Vorräte
        sie protestieren nicht
    wir mauern die Eingänge ihrer Häuser zu
        sie rütteln nicht an den Türen
    wir vergiften ihr Trinkwasser
        sie singen hinter den Fenstern

Ich gehe fort
        Vorher aber
        werde ich noch von ihrem Wasser trinken

The Beaten Conqueror

I come not alone
but as one of a multitude
    we comb the forests
    cross the rivers
    set fire to their sampans
    dynamite their underground system of tunnels
    occupy the town
        they yield without a fight
    we take away their weapons
        they put up no resistance
    we confiscate their supplies
        they make no protest
    we wall up the entrances to their dwellings
        they do not shake the doors
    we poison their drinking water
        we hear them singing inside

I shall move on
        but beforehand
        take a drink of their water

Versammlung

Das Auge des Schlächters in der Menge –

    Er teilt mit geübtem Blick
    die Menschen in Schlachtvieh
    und Zuchtreife
sortiert sie beiläufig
    nach Gewicht Alter und Frische
sein einziger
    Wunsch ist es
    sie hängen zu sehen
        rosigen Fleisches
mit dem Kopf nach unten
gevierteilt
im Ohrlappen das lila Zeichen
des Gottes

    Als sein Mörderblick auf mich fällt
    spüre ich seine Verachtung
    das Messer bleibt ungeöffnet:
    Mich übergibt er dem Abdecker

The Gathering

The eye of the butcher in the throng—

With his trained glance
he sorts people
into cattle for slaughter
and breeding stock
separates them in passing
according to age, condition, avoirdupois
his single-minded
desire:
to see them hanging
head down
bearing the indelible mark of the god
on each ear

As his blood-thirsty glance comes to rest on me
I sense his disdain
his knife remains in its sheath
he abandons me to the knacker

Deutsche Bibliothek Frankfurt am Main

Hier ist alles aufgezeichnet
in deiner Sprache
jedes Wort
das neu geschrieben wird
ist eine Wiederholung
der Wiederholung der Wiederholung

Alle Worte
in Bücher eingeschlossen
in Regalen geordnet
übereinandergeschichtet
neunzehn Stockwerke hoch fensterlos

Immer Geräusche
das Papier trocknet
die Worte zerfallen
in Asche

German Library in Frankfurt

Here everything is registered
in your own language
every word
that is freshly written
is a repetition
of a repetition of a repetition

All the words
enclosed in books
packed side by side
on shelves arranged in tiers
nineteen stories high and no windows

Sounds without end
the pages grow parched
the words turn
into ashes

Nach dem Zitat

Vergiß nicht die Astern
zu ordnen in der Vase
und die Wörter –
die Sätze sind ohne Wiederkehr
wir lauschen
den versickernden Lauten
jedes Echo erstickt
in den Mauern
den frischgekalkten

Zwischen dir und mir
offen
die Wortscharten

A Case in Point

Do not forget
to arrange the asters in the vase
and the words—
our sentences never return
we listen
as the syllables ebb away
and every echo is stifled
in the freshly whitewashed
walls

Between you and me
gaping
chasms of words

Bakunin oder Die Anarchie der Wörter

Wir sind angekommen in der Stadt
es war September und
es regnete leicht
so vergehen die Sätze
so verblassen die Wörter
Gegenwart war einmal und jetzt
        ist die Zukunft schon Vergangenheit
die gleichen Wörter und die anderen Bedeutungen
es bleibt der Zweifel
(zum Beispiel der Zweifel und vor allem der Zweifel)
mehr davon wir lernen nicht aus
die gleichen Bilder und die anderen Bedeutungen
es bleiben die Wörter die Bilder

Angekommen in einer Stadt
unaufgefordert
        uneingeladen
                ungekannt
wir erforschen die Straßen
wir erkunden die Parks
wir entdecken die Kneipen
wir frieren in Hotelzimmern
wir langweilen uns beim Zeitungslesen
wir schlafen in schlechtgelüfteten Kinos
wir verraten uns im Blick eines Uhrenverkäufers
wir begraben uns mit der Dunkelheit der Stadt

Wir finden Zeichen
        wir vernehmen Signale
ein gebrochener Zweig ist etwas vertrautes
ein ankommender Bus
        mit Arbeitern vollgestopft aus den Vorstädten

Bakunin or the Anarchy of Words

We arrived in town
it was September and
there was a light shower
thus the sentences dissolve
and the words fade
the present is no more
            the future has already become the past
identical words with other meanings
doubt remains
(doubt for example, and doubt first and foremost)
            more thereof, we never cease to learn
the same metaphors with other meanings
the words and metaphors remain

Having entered a town
unbidden
            uninvited
                        unknown
we explore its streets
investigate its parks
pick our way to the taverns
freeze in hotel bedrooms
kill time reading newspapers
drowse off in stuffy cinemas
behave suspiciously in the eyes of a watch salesman
bury ourselves in the darkness of the town

We discover signs
            pick up signals
a broken twig is something familiar
a bus full of workers
            arrives from the suburbs

eine Kastanie die aufplatzt
eine Versammlung von Neugierigen
das Heulen einer Polizeisirene
        die Spülung eines Klosetts
the cry of the people for meat
die Geräusche machen es daß wir nicht versinken
daß wir nicht aufgeben
        daß wir nicht sterben
wir gehen am Abend auf die Straßen
wir rufen
        wir fragen in den Bibliotheken
wir suchen bei den Uhrenarbeitern
im Syndikat
        in den Gaststuben
                in den Pissoirs
wir erreichen ihn nicht
wir geben unsere Gesten preis
wir sehen aus den Fenstern des Terminus
da ist nichts als Zukunft die blanke Zukunft
allein seinen Namen
finden wir auf einem weißen Stein in Bremgarten

Wir bleiben in der Stadt
wir verwalten seine Wörter
die gleichen Wörter und die anderen Bedeutungen
wir sind in der Stadt (Neuchâtel)
es ist September und
es regnet leicht

a chestnut bursts open
a gathering of curious onlookers
the howl of a police siren
          the flushing of a toilet
the cry of the people for meat
the sounds save us from becoming submerged
from giving up
          from dying
we take to the streets in the evening
we cry out
          we inquire at the libraries
we muster the clockmakers
at the syndicate
          in the tap-rooms
               in the urinals
and never find him
our activities give us away
staring out of the windows at the terminal
we see nothing but the future, which is blank
all we discover
is his name on a white slab in Bremgarten

We stay on in town
looking after his words
identical words with other meanings
we are in Neuchâtel
it is September
and there is a light shower

Anweisung für Zeitungsleser

I

Prüft jedes Wort
prüft jede Zeile
    vergeßt niemals
    man kann
    mit einem Satz
    auch den Gegen-Satz ausdrücken

II

Mißtraut den Überschriften
den fettgedruckten
    sie verbergen das Wichtigste
mißtraut den Leitartikeln
den Inseraten
den Kurstabellen
den Leserbriefen
und den Interviews am Wochenende

Auch die Umfragen der Meinungsforscher
    sind manipuliert
die Vermischten Nachrichten
    von findigen Redakteuren erdacht
Mißtraut dem Feuilleton
    den Theaterkritiken Die Bücher
    sind meist besser als ihre Rezensenten
lest das was sie verschwiegen haben
Mißtraut auch den Dichtern
    bei ihnen hört sich alles
    schöner an auch zeitloser
aber es ist nicht wahrer nicht gerechter

Directions for Reading the Newspaper

I

Check every word
check every line
    never forget
    that any sentence
    can also be made
    to express the opposite

II

Distrust the headlines
the heavy print
    they obscure essentials
distrust the leaders
    the advertisements
    the market quotations
    the letters to the editor
and the weekend interviews

The public opinion polls
    are also manipulated
the miscellaneous items
    are concocted by slick editors
distrust the cultural section
    the theater reviews. Books
    are usually better than their reviewers
read what the latter ignore
Likewise distrust the poets
    who make everything sound better than it is
    and less time-bound
without getting closer to the truth or to justice

III

Übernehmt nichts
ohne es geprüft zu haben
nicht die Wörter und nicht die Dinge
nicht die Rechnung und nicht das Fahrrad
nicht die Milch und nicht die Traube
nicht den Regen und nicht die Sätze
faßt es an schmeckt es dreht es nach allen Seiten
nehmt es wie eine Münze zwischen die Zähne
hält es stand? taugt es? seid ihr zufrieden?

IV

Ist Feuer noch Feuer und Laub noch Laub
ist Flugzeug Flugzeug und Aufstand Aufstand
ist eine Rose noch eine Rose noch eine Rose?

Hört nicht auf
                euren Zeitungen zu mißtrauen
                auch wenn die Redakteure
                oder Regierungen wechseln

III

Accept nothing
before you have checked it
neither words nor objects
neither a bill nor a bicycle
neither milk nor wine
neither rain nor propositions
feel everything, taste it, inspect it from all sides
take it between your teeth like a coin
is it genuine? is it any good? are you satisfied with it?

IV

Is fire still fire and foliage still foliage
are aircraft aircraft and revolt revolt
is a rose still a rose still a rose?

Never cease
        to distrust the press
        even after a change of editors or
        the appointment of a new cabinet

THE HOUSE

Der Vertrag

So viel Kleingedrucktes
und Zahlen
die man sonst nur im Wirtschaftsteil
einer Zeitung liest
Das langsame Begreifen
der neuen Wörter: das Erschrecken
Abtretungserklärung Zwischenkreditzins
Auffüllung der Bausparsumme
Grundschuldbestellung Auflassungsvormerkung
Schuldurkunde Hypotheken Globalschuld
(Seit dem Katechismus der Kinderzeit
nicht mehr so viel von Schuld gelesen)

Dabei wollte ich nur
etwas mehr Platz zum Arbeiten

So viel Kleingedrucktes
Nichts als Erschrecken
Verträge die niemand verträgt.

The Agreement

So much small print
with statistics
as in the business section
of a newspaper
The gradual comprehension of the meaning
of unfamiliar terms: the panic
subrogation assignment, interim loan interest,
replenishing of the investment with the building society,
registration of the land charge, memorandum of conveyance,
debt certificate, mortgages, global amount due
(Never since bible class in childhood
have I had to read so much of the day of reckoning)

And all I wanted
was a little more elbow-room to work in

So much small print
Sheer panic
Agreements that are so disagreeable to all.

Das Fundament

Im Herbst
fingen sie mit dem Aushub an
Als der erste Schnee taute
blinkten blaue Spiegel aus den Löchern
Woche für Woche fuhr ich hinaus
die Färbung der Erde beobachtend
und die Signale der Jahreszeiten

An einem heißen Julitag
stand dann ein Mann aus Anatolien dort
er schichtete rhythmisch Mörtel auf Stein
seine Lieder füllten die Baugrube

Erst jetzt verstand ich
wie schwer es ist
(und daß es seine Zeit braucht)
das Fundament eines Hauses
nicht nur mit Beton
auch mit Freude aufzurichten

The Foundation

In the fall
they began excavating
When the first snow had melted
blue mirrors glittered in the dug pits
every week I drove out
observing nature's changing tints
and the signals of the seasons

One hot day in July
a man from Anatolia was standing there
rhythmically mortaring bricks
his singing filled the whole site

Now at last I realized
how hard it is
(and that it needs time)
to lay the foundation of a house
not only with concrete
but also with joy

Die Treppe

Der Sommer war trocken
und doch: das Fundament des Hauses
ist mit Wasser angefüllt
unsicher alles und trügerisch

Die Wände sind hochgezogen
aber kein Dach gibt Vertrauen

Gestern haben sie eine
Steintreppe eingebaut
ich weiß nicht
ob sie nach oben
oder nach unten führt

The Staircase

It has been a dry summer
yet the foundation of the house
has filled up with water
everything is precarious, illusive

The walls have been erected
but there is no roof to instill confidence

Yesterday they put in
a stone staircase
I cannot tell
whether it goes up
or down

Einzug in den Neubau

Überall Bücherkisten unausgepackt
das Staunen des Trägers:
›Wenns des ois glesn ham
miaßatns an so an großn Kopf ham‹
Die Abweisung durch leere Wände
Zellenangst
Die nichtvertrauten Räume

Schritte die leiser werden
mit jedem Möbelstück
das neu aufgestellt wird
Die Katze die sich im Schrank
geborgen hat im sichren Geruch
von Schweiß und Haut

Draußen das Ungewisse –
Ich gehe Bier holen

Wenn der Abend kommt
sind die Möbelträger fort
die Freunde die Helfer
die Stille wächst laut
sperrt mich ein
in die Wände kalkweiß
ins kalte Arbeitslicht
der neuen Deckenstrahler

Kein Platz für Erinnerungen
für Geheimnisse und alte Erzählungen
Unruhig wandre ich durch das Gehäuse
einer noch ungeschriebnen Gegenwart
einer zu schreibenden Zukunft

Moving into the New House

Cartons of books lie around unpacked
the moving man voices surprise:
"Once you've read all that
your knob will have grown enormous"
Exclusion by bare walls
the fear of confinement
the unfamiliar rooms

Footsteps become quieter
with every piece of furniture
that is added
The cat's gone into hiding
in the wardrobe with its reassuring smell
of sweat and skin

Outside is terra incognita
I go off to buy beer

When evening comes
the movers will have left
the friends and helpers
the silence becomes loud
locking me in
between walls as white as a sheet
in the cold functional light
from the new ceiling reflectors

No place for memories
for secrets and old reminiscences
Restless I roam through the shell
of a still uncharted present
of a future yet to be placed on the record

In der Küche
über der Eingangstür
begrüße ich meinen ersten Gast
Eine Spinne spinnt dort ihr Netz
ich bin optimistisch:
hier wird es sich wohnen lassen

Ich werde weiterhin in die Stadt fahren
die Diskussionen in der Isabellastraße
die Gespräche mit den andern
über die Sache und wie sie zu machen ist
Und doch:
die Entfernungen sind größer geworden

Above the door
to the kitchen
I welcome my first visitor
a spider spinning its web there
I am of good cheer:
this will prove a pleasant home

I will drive into town as before
for debates in the Isabellastrasse
for talks with the others
about the affair and how to cope
And yet:
the distances have grown larger.

Die Vermessung

Mit Meßfernrohr und Metermaß
wird der Garten ausgemessen
Pflöcke aus grünem Metall
werden in die Erde eingeschlagen
Maschendraht wird ausgerollt und zugeschnitten
Niemand wehrt sich dagegen
eingezellt zu werden
Der Nachbar grüßt
freundlich über den neuen Zaun

Auch ich helfe mit
und sehe doch
wie es enger wird um uns herum
Ich grabe mit den Händen in der Erde

Noch tagelang trag ich sie
schwarz unter meinen Nägeln

Marking Out the Garden

The garden is marked out
with theodolite and measuring rod,
green metal stakes
are pounded into the soil
and wire netting unrolled and cut to size
Nobody objects
to being fenced in
The neighbor waves amiably
from across the new fence

I pitch in and help
yet cannot fail to see
how everything is closing in on us
My fingers dig into the soil

For days on end the dirt
shows black under my nails

Beim Bilderaufhängen

Was ich gern mache
ist Bilder umzuhängen
Der Antes aus dem Wohnzimmer
steckt sein Fußgesicht
jetzt in den dunklen Kaminraum ·
Der Tête d'Homme von Max Ernst
erzählt mir in der Helle des Flurs
ganz neue und fantastischere Geschichten
Der Klapheck bleibt unbeweglich
Bellmer verschlossen am Tag
erst im Abendlicht
öffnen sich Linien und Lippen
Ob ich den Blick von Janssen (Selbstportrait, 1965)
noch lange aushalte?
Wände mit Bildern sind Landschaften
die ich willkürlich verändere
(meine Schöpfungszeit)
manchmal verurteile ich eine Grafik
von der träumenden Wand
in die lichtlose Mappe
zu Straflager

In meinem Arbeitszimmer
dulde ich nur Bilder die schweigen
und schweigend mir ins Auge sehn
die klar sind und ohne Tiefe
und die beim langen Hinstarrn
nicht anfangen zu reden
Zugegeben: wenige nur gibt es
und auch die hängen hier nicht lange

An dieser Stelle
ist noch ein Platz frei
für einen Albers (oder einen Nicholson):
das wird noch eine Weile dauern
Doch schon jetzt schlage ich
den Nagel dafür in die Wand

Picture-hanging

I have a yen
for picture-hanging
The Antes from the living room
now pokes its foot-face into the dark basement
Max Ernst's *Tête d'homme*
in the well-lit corridor tells me
entirely new and even stranger stories
The Klapheck stays put
Bellmer, unforthcoming all day long,
its lines and lips
part only in the evening light
How long will I still abide
Janssen's gaze (*Self-portrait, 1965*)?
Walls with pictures are landscapes
that I change at will
(my opportunity to be creative)
sometimes I relegate a drawing
from the dreaming wall
to the lightless folder
to the detention camp

In my study
I only suffer pictures that keep mum
and eye me mutely,
that have clarity without depth
and, under my persistent gaze,
never venture to pipe up
Admittedly, they are few in number,
and they, too, are not left hanging for long

Over here
there is still space
for an Albers (or a Nicholson)
though that will have to wait a while
Yet, in anticipation, I already knock an appropriate nail
into the wall

Die Katze (Cäsar)

Meine Katze
ist das Denkmal einer Katze
Das Denkmal einer Katze
müßte so sein
wie meine Katze

Manchmal gehe ich ganz nah
an sie heran
und lausche
ob sie noch atmet

The Cat

My cat
is the statue of a cat
The statue of a cat
ought to look
like my cat

Sometimes I move very close to him
to hear
whether he's
still breathing

Gras

Ich grabe die Erde um
der Boden will bereitet sein
für etwas Freundlichkeit
Nur ein paar Disteln laß ich stehn
damit der Weg nicht allzuglatt sei
sie teiln Erinnerung aus:
ich hatte schlechtere Zeiten
ich vergeß es nicht

Ich säe das Gras
streue den Samen
in den Wind
Meine Hand träumt vom Grün
einer ungewissen Zukunft
Noch kleben die Spelzen im Mund
und der Regen versteckt
sich hinter der Gartentür

Ich seh es wachsen
seh die Verwandlung von Rauch
und Asche und Stickstoff und
manch nichtgeschriebner Sätze
sehe es draußen wachsen
das Fahnengrün
freundlich
überm Boden gehißt

Grass

I turn up the soil
the ground has to be prepared
for a little friendliness
All I leave standing are a few clumps of thistles
so that the path will not be too smooth
these evoke memories:
I have known worse times
that I will not forget

I sow the grass
scattering the seeds
into the wind
My hand dreams of the greenness
of an indeterminate future
The grain husks still stick in the mouth
and the rain crouches
behind the garden gate

I watch it grow
see the transmutation of smoke,
ash, nitrogen
and some unwritten passages
watch it grow outside
watch the unfurling
of friendly green flags
above the ground

Die Aussicht

Betrachtend die Birke
die vor meinem Fenster sich wiegt
erinnre ich mich an den grünen Rücken
eines indischen Reisbauern
in einem Film von Satyajit Ray
Dahinter der graue Kubus
einer fensterlosen Wand
in die ich nachdenkend
meine Zeichen setze

An der Straßenecke ein violettes Dreieck
das die Geräusche von Todesautos
in meine Träume schickt
Ein blauer Stahlmast
weit entfernt und in gedachter Linie
Signal verordneter Gemeinsamkeit
durchs Fernsehen

Im grünen Lupinefeld tanzende Lampione:
Kinder in gelben Regenumhängen
Und als Begrenzung meines Auges
die weiße Pyramide der Hochhäuser
am Münchner Ring schattenlos
und ohne Perspektive
Marmorwolken über allem
rotgeädert aus Carrara

Ich warte bis alles erstarrt
zu einem Bild von de Chirico
mit mir selbst am Fenster lehnend
bleich und starr und zeitversäumt –
mit Aufschlag auf einer Auktion versteigert

Das langsam vergehende Licht
versammelt sich grün
im Bauch der böhmischen Vase
auf dem Fensterbord

The View

Watching the birch
swaying in front of my window
I recall the green back
of an Indian peasant sowing rice
in a film by Satyajit Ray
In the background the gray cube
of a windowless wall
on which I pensively
leave my mark

At the street corner, a violet triangle
injects the noise of lethal automobiles
into my dreams
Against the skyline
a blue steel repeater tower
for line-of-sight TV transmission
A symbol of regulation community
antenna television

Lanterns dance in the green field of lupines:
children in yellow raincoats
And, obscuring my view,
the white pyramids of the high-rise buildings
along the Münchener Ring, casting no shadows
and with no outlook
Everything covered in clouds
of red-veined Carrara marble

I wait for everything to crystallize
into a Chirico painting
with me leaning out the window
wan, rigid and framed in time—
to be auctioned off to the highest bidder

The gradually fading light
collects as a green glow
in the belly of the Bohemian vase
on the windowsill

Der Arbeitstisch (Am 20. Juni 1973)

Da ist Papier und hier
im Glas die Kugelschreiber
Eine Briefwaage Eine Schere Eine Rolle Tesafilm
Links der Stapel mit Wörterbüchern
Dazwischen Auktionskataloge Der Beckett
in dem ich gerade lese
Unbeantwortete Briefe Korrigierte Manuskriptseiten

Vor mir an der Wand
Arbeitstermine S-Bahn-Zeiten Einladungen
mit Reißnägeln festgemacht
Der Kalender der Hypo-Bank
mit Eintragungen grün und rot
In den Regalen links und rechts
die Briefe ungeordnet
und die Zeitungsausschnitte
Das Telefon weit weggerückt
ist nah wenn Freunde rufen

In der Schreibmaschine
ein leeres weißes Blatt
das mich verwundet

Hier ist Papier und da
der Kugelschreiber
daneben ein Glas Whisky mit viel Wasser
Ich fange an zu schreiben

The Writing Desk (June 20, 1973)

Here is paper and,
in a jar, ball-point pens
Letter scales, scissors, a reel of Scotch tape
On the left a pile of dictionaries
In between, auction catalogues, the Beckett
I am just reading
Mail waiting to be answered, corrected pages of manuscript

On the wall facing me
the dates of deadlines, train schedules, invitations
all secured with thumbtacks
The calendar of the Hypo Bank
with green and red entries
On the shelves to the left and right
unsorted correspondence,
newspaper clippings
The telephone, shoved far aside
is at hand when friends ring up

In the typewriter
a blank sheet of paper
plagues me

Here is paper and there
the ball-point pen
next to it a tumbler of whiskey
with lots of water
I start to write

IN AUSTRALIA

Lern von den Wombats

Weit bin ich gegangen, das ist wahr,
und zurückgekehrt zu den alten Wörtern.
Die Erde. Die Sonne. Das Gras. Die Wüste.
Der Regen. Es gibt Zeiten, in denen er
sich in Wald verwandelt. Die Straßen
dampfen. Die Füße unterm Schreibtisch
fangen zu faulen an. Lerne: schon
im September verrät dich das Licht
an einen messerblitzenden Himmel.

Ich bin noch nicht lange genug hier,
um die bizarren Zeichen der
Ghost-Trees zu enträtseln,
die blauen Tätowierungen
von der Haut wegzuwischen,
die Todesnachrichten beim Grillfeuer
zu lesen. Lerne vom Licht, vom Regen
und von den erdhaften Wombats.

Learn from the Wombats

I have come a long way, it is true,
and found my way back to the old words.
Soil. Sun. Grass. Desert.
Rain. There are times
when it turns into trees. Vapor
rises from the streets. Under the desk my feet
fall asleep. Know that by September
the light will expose you
to a sky of flashing knives.

I have not been here long enough
to decipher the peculiar pictograms
of the ghost trees,
to wipe the blue tattoo marks
off the skin,
to read the obituaries in the light of the barbecue fire.
Learn from the light, from the rain
and from the burrowing wombats.

Unterwegs

Wörter. Nichts als Wörter.

Aber die Zeugenschaft der Bäume.
Gum Trees. Eukalyptus. Geisterbäume.
Lies in den Zweigen. Lies die Rinde!
Schwarz die verbrannten Stümpfe. Waldrebus.

Zähle die Feuer. Zähle die Feuer!

Under Way

Words. Nothing but words.

But the testimony of the trees.
Gum trees. Eucalyptus. Ghost trees. /
Read the twigs. Read the bark!
Stumps burnt black. Rebus in the woods.

Count the fires. Count the fires!

Lake Eyre

Niemals sah ich Sonne und Mond
so nah zusammen wie dort am Eyre-See
auf dem Weg von Leigh-Creek nach Oodnadatta.
Das weiße blendende Salz vom Eyre-See
hat unsre Augen gepfählt und den Horizont
zerschnitten. (Hier werden sonst
die schnellsten Autorennen der Welt gefahren;
hier gibt es Wasser nur alle hundert Jahre.)
Aus dem weißen Gerippe eines Pferdes
läßt sich nicht die Zukunft herauslesen,
ich weiß es. Und doch gehn wir mit dem
schwarzhäutigen *Aboriginal* zur Feuerstelle
und sehn zu wie er mit glühendem Draht
in einen Knochen magische Zeichen brennt,
die wir mühsam enträtseln:

Wenn du dein Herz herausreißt, Bruder,
und es dampfend in die salzige Sonne hältst,
wird der See mit Wasser anschwellen
und den Mond herunterziehn, tief,
und fruchtbar wird das Land, ringsum.

Weitergefahren sind wir, erschreckt.
Darüber hab ich früher in alten Büchern gelesen.
(Sammlung Diederich.) Und es niemals geglaubt. –
Das Salz zerbiß unsre Haut und trieb
weiße Kristalle aus unseren Augen.
Noch heute finde ich Spuren davon
in der Achselhöhle, unterm Skrotum, zwischen den Zehen.

Und ich denke daran, mit etwas mehr Mut
wär ich es vielleicht gewesen,
der einmal Sonne und Mond vereint hätte,
dort im gleißenden Salzlicht vom Eyre-See.
Glaub an die Bücher!

Lake Eyre

Never have I seen sun and moon
closer together than at Lake Eyre
on the way from Leigh Creek to Oodnadatta.
The glaring white salt of Lake Eyre
impaled our eyes, diffracted
the skyline. (This is otherwise the site
of the world's fastest motor races,
the lake being dry save for once in a hundred years.)
The future cannot be foretold
from the bleached bones of a horse,
of that I am aware. Yet we follow
the black-skinned aboriginal to the fire
and witness how, with a red hot wire,
he burns magical signs into a bone
which we laboriously interpret:

Pluck out your heart, brother,
and hold it up, steaming, in the salty sun
then the lake will fill with water
and draw the moon down very close
and the land all around will become fertile.

We traveled on, disquieted.
All this I had read about in old books
(Diederich's Miscellany). And believed not a word.—
The salt bit into our skins, forced
white crystals out of our eyes.
To this day I still find material evidence
under my armpits, scrotum and between my toes.

And I reflect that, with a bit more nerve,
it might have been me
who untied the sun and moon
there in the glaring saline light of Lake Eyre.
Lend credence to the books.

Sydney Opera House

Ikarus stürzte ins Meer. So
haben wirs in der Schule gelernt.
Jetzt erst weiß ich: es kann nicht weit
von Bennelong-Point gewesen sein. Hier
ist er aus dem Wasser gestiegen, triumphierend,
mit hundert Flügeln und zwölf Segeln
(gleißend weiß und geschuppt)
von einem trotzigen Dänen versteint,
kühn ins Meer wie in den Himmel
getrieben –
bis allen schwindlig davon wurde.

Dämmerzeit, in der sich dies Land
die Augen reibt und erschreckt
etwas von seiner eigenen Kühnheit
zu ahnen beginnt. Im blauen Oktoberlicht.
Die eine Sprache
und die vielen Zungen.

Wenn das Licht ausgeht im Konzertsaal
werden die Erinnerungen hell.
Schönberg: A Survivor from Varsaw, op. 46 (1947)
Mahler: Symphonie No. 5 C sharp minor
Und in der Pause ziehn hier in Rufweite
die haushohen *Oceanliner* vorbei.

Leg dies Blatt beiseite und sag mir:
Wo in der Welt, wo, siehst du das sonst?

Sydney: The Opera House

Icarus plonked into the sea. So
we were told at school.
Now it dawns upon me: it must have been
hard by Bennelong Point. There
he emerged from the waves, triumphant,
with a hundred wings and a dozen sails
(glistening white and bedecked with scales)
built in stone by a wilful Dane,
and extending boldly
into both sea and sky
so that all our heads were swimming

The time around dawn, when this country
rubs its eyes and, with a start,
begins to grasp the extent of its daring.
In October's bluish light.
A single language
but many tongues.

When the lights are dimmed in the concert hall
memories become lucid.
Schönberg: A Survivor from Warsaw, op. 46 (1947)
Mahler: Symphony No. 5, C sharp minor
And during the interval the giant ocean liners
glide past within calling distance.

Lay this page aside and tell me:
Where else in the world are such sights to be witnessed.

Ausflug nach Wollongong

In den bizarren Bauten der
Kompaß-Termiten les ich,
daß meine Zeit hier
befristet ist.
Ungewißheiten.

Wie im alten Europa.

Excursion to Wollongong

From the strange structures of the
compass-termites I note that
a time limit has been set
to my sojourn here.
Insecurities.

As in old Europe.

Under the Southern Cross

Fremantle. Perth. Und Sydney.
Ja Sydney! The Great Railway Line.
Und Brisbane. Ach, verdammtes Brisbane.
Melbourne: Vor lauter Häßlichkeit versunken.
Nicht wiedergefunden, weil
keiner danach suchte: Tasmania. Weit.
Herz aus Sand: Alice Springs.

Alles entdeckt, erforscht, begangen.
Mit ANSETT unterwegs. Den Reiseführer unterm Arm.
Expeditionen nurmehr nachts,
übern südlichen Himmel. Ja. Das Kreuz
des Südens! Ah! Sterne und Sätze.
Der Centaurus. Indus. Crux und
Corona Australis. Ah, ah. Ein Staunen,
das nicht aufhören will.
Unterm Wendekreis des Steinbocks.

Dabei such ich Cepheus. Die Geliebte des
Großen Bären. Andromeda. Cassiopeia,
die Vertraute. Heimat. Und die Oder, die Weichsel,
ganz unten, ein Kindertraum. Swięta Maryja,
mòdl się za nami grzesznymi. Sieh nach unten!
Nach unten! Berühr die Erde mit deinen Händen.
Die rote Erde Australiens.

Mahl die Wahrheit zwischen den Zähnen,
lange, wie Sand; Sand. Spuck ihn aus, Woomera-rot.
Die Wahrheit: von hier ist *alles* fern.

Under the Southern Cross

Fremantle. Perth. And Sydney.
Yes, Sydney! The Great Southern Railway line
And Brisbane. Ah, damnable Brisbane.
Melbourne immersed in sheer ugliness.
Never rediscovered because
no one ever undertook a search: Tasmania.
Heart made of sand: Alice Springs.

All discovered, explored, trekked.
Under way with Ansett. The tourist guide clamped under the arm.
Expeditions now only at night
across the southern sky. Yes, the Southern
Cross! Ah, stars and propositions.
Centaurus. Indus. Crux and
Corona Australis. Ah, ah. Wonders
without cease.
Under the Tropic of Capricorn.

I look out in vain for familiar stars: Cepheus,
husband of Andromeda. Cassiopeia.
On home ground: the Oder, the Vistula,
right down under, a childhood dream. Święta Marya,
modl się za nami grzesznymi. Look down under.
Down under! Let your hands touch the soil.
The red soil of Australia.

Grind the truth between your teeth
for an eternity, like sand. Spit out the red Woomera sand.
In truth: everywhere is far from here.

Voss, auch Leichhardt geheißen

Auf den Spuren
von Voss, der Leichhardt geheißen
und aus dem finsteren Deutschland kam.
Dunkel ists jetzt auch in Sarsaparilla.
Hinter den weißen Rolläden tickt
die Schreibmaschine des Aus-Gezeichneten.
Seine Einsamkeit ist noch größer geworden.

On the road. Braun wird die Erde,
rot, und schließlich lilafarben,
unsere Augen weiß, kranichweiß.
Seine letzte Nachricht in Laubschrift
vom dritten April 1848,
als zuhaus schon die ersten Herrenhäuser
brannten. Dieses ›wissende irre Lachen‹,
das Patrick White an ihm beschreibt.

Was man jetzt hier findet,
ist verbrannt, verkohlt, ausgeglüht,
dein Herz, Bruder, malt
mit den schwarzen Farben von Dubbo
den Himmel herunter, löscht ihn aus.

Jetzt zerfallen die Straßen in Staub
und wir sind nichts weiter als
eine gelbe lodernde Sandfackel.

Vielleicht, denk ich, sollte ich
einmal Stifter lesen, Abdias, Zwei Schwestern.
›Das Wehen der Luft, das Rieseln des Wassers,
das Wachsen des Getreides . . . ist groß‹
– aufblitzt am Hals das Rasiermesser.

Nullarbor. Wiederhol das: Nullarbor.

Voss, also known as Leichhardt

On the trail
of Voss, real name Leichhardt
who came from darkest Germany.
Darkness has since also descended on Sarsaparilla.
Hacking away behind white roll-up blinds
the typewriter of the en-Nobeled author.
His isolation has become even greater.

On the road. The soil turns brown,
red and ultimately a pinkish-mauve,
our eyes are white, the color of cranes.
His last message written in the leaves
on April 2, 1848
when, back in the Fatherland, the first manor houses
were going up in flames. His "knowing wild laughter"
that Patrick White described.

What we find here now
is burnt, charred, reduced to dust,
your heart, brother, applies
the somber pigments of Dubbo
to black out the sky.

Here the roads crumble to dust
and we are nothing but
a blazing torch of yellow sand.

Perhaps, I ruminate, I ought
to read Stifter's *Abdias, Two Sisters.*
"The wafts of air, the trickle of water,
the growing grain . . . is great."
—the razor flashing at the throat.

Nullarbor. Repeat: Nullarbor.

Ein Wort so groß, um ein Gedicht
drin zu verstecken für einen für dich
für niemand. Nullarbor,
singt die Luft, rieselt das Wasser,
wächst das Getreide. Nullarbor.
Und Alexander übersetzt es: *Kein Baum.*

Wenn er das Wort gekannt hätte . . .
Die brennenden Herrenhäuser in Deutschland
wären ihm lieber gewesen als
die flammenden Horizonte der
Großen Simpson-Wüste. Vielleicht
hat er sie noch gesehn – Nullarbor,
als die Sichel im Hals aufblitzte,
geschwungen von einem trance-verzückten *Aboriginal.*

Fahr uns weiter, schwarzer Jackie, Nachfahr,
mit dem ANSETT-Bus 4216,
On the Tracks of Voss,
der Ludwig Leichhardt geheißen.

A word so large one can stash
a poem in it for someone, for you,
for no one. The air sings
Nullarbor, the water trickles,
the grain grows. Nullarbor.
Alexander translated it: *No Tree*.

Had the word but been known to him . . .
The burning manor houses in Germany
would have appealed to him more
than the fiery horizon
of the vast Simpson Desert. Perhaps
he even set foot there—Nullarbor,
as the sickle flashed at his throat
swung by an aborigine in a trance.

Drive on, Black Jackie, descendant,
with the Ansett bus 4216.
On the trail of Voss,
real name Ludwig Leichhardt.

Sydney, im Juni

1788 gegründet, rund drei
Millionen Einwohner, heute.
›An einer der schönsten Buchten
der Welt gelegen‹, Brockhaus, 1933.
Für mich ist es die schönste: Port Jackson.
Und diese Bays zwischen den *Skyscrapers!*
Bondi. Manly. Coogee. Rose. Double.
Und die Inszenierung Paddington.

Ach ja, Paddington. Als ob Magritte
durch ein Bühenbild spazierte. Mit schwarzer
Melone. Und der Hemdenverkäufer in Oxford-Street,
der die neuen, noch ungewohnten Wörter
mit schwarzen Sonnenblumenkernen ausspuckt;
auf seiner goldnen Armkette blitzt noch
die Sonne Apuliens. Ich lasse nicht
von seinen Augen. La terra promessa.

Dann: The Harbour Bridge. The Rocks.
Australian Square Tower. Cenotaph.
The Opera House, ja. Kings Cross.
The Yellow House. Macquarie Place. Taronga.
Old Mint. Waratah. Ja, Waratah! Und Randwick.
Ich probiere die neuen Wörter.

Ich möchte sie schützend
wie ein Dach
über meine Verlorenheit ziehen.

Sydney in June

Founded 1788, present population
about three million.
"Situated on one of the world's
most picturesque bays," Brockhaus, 1933.
To me it is *the* most picturesque: Port Jackson.
And those bays between the skyscrapers!
Bondi. Manly. Coogee. Rose. Double.
And the street spectacle of Paddington.

Ah, yes. Paddington. As though Magritte
had appeared upon the scene. Wearing a black
bowler. And the shirt-salesman in Oxford Street
spitting out new, still unfamiliar words
along with black sunflower seeds:
his gold bracelet still reflecting
the Apuleian sun. I keep my eyes
trained on his. La terra promessa.

Then: Harbour Bridge. The Rocks.
The Square Tower. The Cenotaph.
The Opera House, yes. King's Cross.
The Yellow House. Macquarie Place. Taronga.
The Old Mint. Waratah. Yes, Waratah! And Randwick.
I savor the new words.

I would like to draw them like a canopy
for protection
over my forlorn self.

Hinter den Blitzen

Nimm die Hand vom Papier
leg den Kugelschreiber beiseite
unterbrich die sich allzurasch
füllenden Zeilen geh hin geh hin
und sprich noch einmal langsam leis
die früh erlernten Wörter nach:
das Gras und die Wiese
der Baum und die Rinde
der Fluß und die Wasser
der Stein und die Binse
das Feuer die Wahrheit
der Rauch die Vogelbeere
Skarbnik der Berggeist *Pitwok* das Spiel
mit dem Messer *Pulok* Spiele der Kindheit
Der Knabenteich Die brennenden Königskerzen
an den Bahndämmen und am Rand der Chausseen
Abendlicht auf blauen Lupinen tanzt

Beschreib die Räusche Geräusche im August
in den Kornfeldern im Haar und im Mund
da alles was sich bewegt den Sommer preist
und heiter kommt der Tod mit den
polnischen Schnittern über die Grenze singend
Strach ist die Angst Die Stoppeln
peitschen blutig deine Füße auf der Flucht
Auf der Flucht vor der Kindheit
die Wälder schrein und die Flüsse schwelln an
die Wolken jagen über den Fördertürmen hin
Wind aus dem Osten die Feuer kommen zurück
Utopletz holt die Kinder *Strach*
Flieh vor der Angst Such den Stein das Wort
und die Wahrheit im Flußwehr Wasser steigen und fallen

Lob du die Glut ich lobe das Feuer
wer zu uns gehört redet in Flammen
geh hin schreib das auf leg die Hand aufs Papier
Aus der Heimat hinter den Blitzen rot
Da kommen die Wolken her,
Aber Vater und Mutter sind lange tot,
Es kennt mich dort keiner mehr

Beyond the Sheet Lightning

Withdraw your hand from the paper
lay aside the ball-point pen
halt the over-hurried
flow of words, go off, go off
to intone once more, softly and slowly,
words learnt as a child
grass and meadow
tree and bark
river and lakes
fire and truth
smoke, rowanberries
skarbnik the spirit guardian of hill and mine
pitwok the penknife used in play
pulok frolics of boyhood
the old water hole, blazing goldenrods
along railway embankments and highways
the evening light dancing over blue lupines

Record the delights of August
in cornfields hair and mouth
when all that stirs celebrates the summer
and death comes blithely across the border
with the Polish reapers singing their songs
strach strikes fear, stubble
bloodies one's feet in headlong flight
In flight from childhood
the woods cry out, the rivers swell
clouds race across the sky above the derrick towers
An east wind blows, the fires are returning
The *utopliec* goes for the children, *strach*
Flee from fear, search for the stone, for the word
and veracity in the river dam
Waters rise and fall
You praise the embers, I the fire
our kind converse in tongues of flame
the clouds appear from way back home
beyond the flashes red
but I would be a stranger there
now father and mother are long dead

Notes on the Poems

Page 15   A Day
Ostrog: a Russian labor camp.
purga: a polar snowstorm.

Page 17   Katorga
Katorga: Russian for "forced labor."

Page 19   The Shots at Noon
The coalmining area of Vorkuta, which lies between the Arctic Sea and the Northern Urals, was, under Stalin, one of the most notorious places of punishment for political prisoners from all over Europe. After the fall of Beria in 1953, a strike broke out, which after eleven days was bloodily suppressed, around noon on 1 August. Since then the prisoners have been pardoned, but some of them have been forced to settle in the area.

Page 61   Our Ashes
black wall: the wall against which shootings were carried out in Auschwitz.

Page 65   Signs and Propositions
Line 13: Wittgenstein, *Tractatus Logico-Philosophicus.*

Page 69   Boyhood in Gleiwitz
1 *Pistulka:* a legendary outlaw of the Gleiwitz region.
2 The local broadcast was interrupted by shots around 20 hours on August 31, 1939, when a group of six SS men under the command of Sturmbannführer Alfred Naujocks simulated a Polish attack on the Gleiwitz radio station. The German SS commandos wore Polish army uniforms and were equipped with Polish weapons, all supplied by Admiral Canaris, head of German Intelligence. This incident was used by Hitler as a pretext for the invasion of Poland on September 1, 1939.
3 *pulok:* Silesian Polish slang for penis.
4 *dupa:* Polish slang for arse with the additional meaning of idiot.
5 During the winter offensive of the Red Army, the surviving inmates of Auschwitz (Polish: Oświęim) Concentration Camp, referred to as "stripies" because of their striped prison garb, were marched in columns into the interior of Germany. On January 19, 1945, some of these columns passed through Gleiwitz, which is situated no more than about 25 miles from the concentration camp.

6 As the vast German army was swept out of Russia and Poland during the fall of 1945, hundreds of thousands of Silesian Germans, including the inhabitants of Gleiwitz, fled on foot into the interior of Germany.

7 *Bezchlebia*: a small, sparsely populated area near Gleiwitz with numerous gravel and sand pits. It was renamed "Laband" by the Germans during World War II.

8 This and subsequent italicized lines of verse are slight variations on a poem, "Die zwei Gesellen" ("The Two Journeymen"), by the Upper Silesian poet Joseph von Eichendorff (1788-1857), which was first printed in 1818.

9 Jan Hus, the Czech religious reformer, was burned at the stake for heresy in 1415 under Pope John XXIII.

10 A Polish term of endearment for the river Klodka also used by Silesian Germans; the German name of the river was Klodnitz.

11 Silesian Germans with Polish names were being pressured to adopt German names.

12 RAW was the abbreviation of "Reichsbahn Ausbesserungswerk."

13 *mćj Boża kochana*: Polish for "My dear God."

14 The "SPEAK GERMAN" signs were put up by the Germans to discourage bilingual Silesians from speaking Polish.

15 *Sieg*: German for "victory."

16 *Perunnja*: a mild Polish imprecation also widely used by Silesian Germans. Perun is the old Slavic god of thunder.

17 *Calvary*: a reference to Góra Swiętej Anny (German: Annaberg), a place of pilgrimage.

Page 101 Shadow Language

Lines 11-13: Wittgenstein, *Tractatus Logico-Philosophicus*, 5.4711.

Page 155 Voss, also known as Leichhardt

Ludwig Leichhardt was a German naturalist who disappeared without a trace during his attempt in 1848 to be the first human being to cross Australia from east to west. Patrick White, who was awarded the 1973 Nobel Prize for Literature, wrote a novel about Leichhardt under the title *Voss*. In the novel, Voss is killed by an aboriginal.

Sarsaparilla: a town invented by White for another novel. It is supposed to be located in the region of Sydney, which is the scene of most of his novels.

Beyond the Sheet Lightning

Skarbnik: in Polish folklore, a spirit guardian of a sacred hill or mine concealing a treasure or natural wealth such as minerals, often a coal mine. In everyday Polish the word means "treasurer."

Pitwok: a colloquial Silesian word of Wendish origin meaning a knife.

Pulok: Silesian Polish slang for penis.

Strach: in Polish folklore, a scarifying specter that haunts ancient castles, low taverns, huts, attics, chapels, ravines, etc. In everyday Polish the word means both "fear" and "specter."

Utopliec (pron. u-top-lyetz): also commonly called a topielec. In Slavic folklore, a water sprite living in lakes, rivers, wells. He has fish eyes, green teeth and red legs or stockings. Traditionally he brings the newborn babies like the proverbial stork, but is also known to lure people into the water in order to pull them down until they drown. In everyday Polish the word is reflected in the verb *utopić*, meaning "to drown."

Skarbnik: in Polish folklore, a spirit guardian of a sacred hill or mine concealing a treasure of natural wealth such as minerals, often a coal mine. In everyday Polish the word means "treasurer".

Pszcoca: a colloquial Silesian word of Wendish origin meaning a knife.

Fiuki: Silesian Polish slang for penis.

Strzyca: in Polish folklore, a terrifying specter that haunts ancient castles, lone taverns, huts, attics, chapels, ravines, etc. In everyday Polish the word means both "fear" and "specter".

Utopiec (pan u-top-yets): also commonly called a topielec. In Slavic folklore, a water sprite living in lakes, rivers, wells. He has fish eyes, green teeth and red legs or stockings. Traditionally he brings the newborn babies like the proverbial stork, but is also known to lure people into the water in order to pull them down until they drown. In everyday Polish the word is reflected in the verb utopić, meaning "to drown".

Biographical Notes

HORST BIENEK was born in 1930 in Gleiwitz, Upper Silesia (now Poland), the town on the Polish border where the attack on the radio station, organized by the Nazis, unleashed the invasion of Poland and the beginning of World War II.

His ancestors were both Polish, from his mother's side, and German, from his father's side—both, however, were Catholic. So he spent his childhood between the Don Bosco League, the Hitler Youth Organization and Catholic May services.

After the war, Bienek worked with Bertolt Brecht in the Berliner Ensemble in East Berlin. There he was arrested in 1951 and sentenced to twenty-five years hard labor by a Soviet military court. He survived four years in a Stalinist slave-labor camp, Vorkuta, in the notorious Gulag Archipelago, a life he dramatized in his first novel, *Die Zelle* (*The Cell*, Unicorn Press, 1972). He was pardoned after Stalin's death.

Horst Bienek has been living in the Federal Republic of Germany since 1956, and he has been publishing poems, stories, novels, essays and interviews. His most ambitious and recent work is the tetralogy, GLEIWITZ QUARTET, four novels being released one by one by Atheneum. *Time Without Bells*, the third novel of the four, was brought out in 1988. The tetralogy is being translated into seven languages.

Unicorn Press introduced Bienek in its UNICORN GERMAN SERIES in 1968, a volume reprinted by Penguin in their MODERN EUROPEAN POETRY SERIES in England. Bienek now lives in Munich, West Germany. In 1985 he visited the United States as poet-in-residence at Tulane University.

HANS BENDER, born in 1919, is one of the leading literary critics of the avant garde in Germany.

MATTHEW MEAD, born in England, has lived with his wife, Ruth, born in Germany, in Bonn for the past twenty years.

EVA HESSE grew up in Germany and England. She is the German translator of Ezra Pound, Robinson Jeffers, and T.S. Eliot. She is also well-known as an essayist.